"The Object Lessons series achieves something very close to magic: the books take ordinary—even banal—objects and animate them with a rich history of invention, political struggle, science, and popular mythology. Filled with fascinating details and conveyed in sharp, accessible prose, the books make the everyday world come to life. Be warned: once you've read a few of these, you'll start walking around your house, picking up random objects, and musing aloud: 'I wonder what the story is behind this thing?'"

Steven Johnson, author of *Where Good Ideas Come From* and *How We Got to Now*

"Object Lessons describes themselves as 'short, beautiful books,' and to that, I'll say, amen. . . . If you read enough Object Lessons books, you'll fill your head with plenty of trivia to amaze and annoy your friends and loved ones—caution recommended on pontificating on the objects surrounding you. More importantly, though . . . they inspire us to take a second look at parts of the everyday that we've taken for granted. These are not so much lessons about the objects themselves, but opportunities for self-reflection and storytelling. They remind us that we are surrounded by a wondrous world, as long as we care to look."

John Warner, *The Chicago Tribune*

OBJECTLESSONS

A book series about the hidden lives of ordinary things.

Series Editors:

Ian Bogost and Christopher Schaberg

In association with

BOOKS IN THE SERIES

OK

MICHELLE MCSWEENEY

BLOOMSBURY ACADEMIC
NEW YORK • LONDON • OXFORD • NEW DELHI • SYDNEY

BLOOMSBURY ACADEMIC
Bloomsbury Publishing Inc
1385 Broadway, New York, NY 10018, USA
50 Bedford Square, London, WC1B 3DP, UK
29 Earlsfort Terrace, Dublin 2, Ireland

BLOOMSBURY, BLOOMSBURY ACADEMIC and the Diana logo are trademarks
of Bloomsbury Publishing Plc

First published in the United States of America 2023

Copyright © Michelle McSweeney, 2023

Cover Design: Alice Marwick

Bloomsbury Publishing Inc does not have any control over, or responsibility for, any third-party
websites referred to or in this book. All internet addresses given in this book were correct at the
time of going to press. The author and publisher regret any inconvenience caused if addresses
have changed or sites have ceased to exist, but can accept no responsibility for any such changes.

A catalogue record for this book is available from the British Library

Library of Congress Cataloging-in-Publication Data

Names: McSweeney, Michelle A., author.
Title: Ok / Michelle McSweeney.
Other titles: Okay
Description: New York : Bloomsbury Academic, 2023. | Series: Object lessons | Includes
bibliographical references and index. | Summary: "OK as a word can agree, accept, inspire, and
describe the world; as an object, OK and its variants (okay, ok, etc.) tell a story about the ways that
technology and globalization change the way we communicate"–Provided by publisher.
Identifiers: LCCN 2022022208 (print) | LCCN 2022022209 (ebook) | ISBN 9781501367182
(paperback) | ISBN 9781501367199 (epub) | ISBN 9781501367205 (pdf) | ISBN 9781501367212
Subjects: LCSH: Okay (The English word)
Classification: LCC PE1599.O33 M44 2023 (print) | LCC PE1599.O33 (ebook) |
DDC 420.1/43–dc23/eng/20220818
LC record available at https://lccn.loc.gov/2022022208
LC ebook record available at https://lccn.loc.gov/2022022209

ISBN: PB: 978-1-5013-6718-2
ePDF: 978-1-5013-6720-5
eBook: 978-1-5013-6719-9

Series: Object Lessons

Typeset by Deanta Global Publishing Services, Chennai, India
Printed and bound in the United States of America

To find out more about our authors and books visit www.bloomsbury.com and
sign up for our newsletters.

Devon and Patrick Valentine, who fill
life with beauty, curiosity, and love <3
And for Nancy, now there's proof
that O.K. was never ok.

CONTENTS

1 OK (INTRODUCTION)

On the morning of March 23, 1839, the English language changed forever. It was an otherwise ordinary day, so unmomentous that even the Farmer's Almanac, which has a note for every day in April, has nothing but fair weather and early morning frost for March 23.[1] But when readers of the *Boston Morning Post* encountered "o. k.—all correct," they were participating in a small act of language change that would have giant impact on language, and not just English. But readers probably thought nothing of it. There were no clues to indicate that the most popular word in the history of the human language had just been invented, and there were lots of other acronyms in the paper that day to distract away from ok. But that's how language change works—no one knows when their little piece of linguistic creativity will catch on and change the world forever.

By all accounts, OK hasn't just caught on—it has become central to how we communicate. It appears in all kinds of

---

[1]Murphey, 1838 (almanacs are printed the year before).

contexts with all kinds of meanings. We can use it to agree with someone (Let's get ice cream! Ok!) but also to imply disagreement (Time to take out the garbage! Ok, but . . .). We can use it to describe something as good (How was your day? It was ok.) and to describe something as bad (How was your day? It was ok.). We can use it to open a monologue (Ok, let's get started), close a conversation (Ok, have a good day!), and change the topic (Ok, how about those Yankees). We can even do all of this and more in one conversation. Take this example:

"Want to go to the movies?"

"OK!"

"OK, let's go!"

[hours later, exiting the theatre]

"OK, what did you think?"

"It was OK, I really liked the twist at the end. What did you think?"

"It was OK, I thought they could have filmed it better"

For just one word, OK has done a lot in this conversation. There is the adverb to express agreement in line 2, the discourse marker to manage the conversational flow in lines 3 and 4, and the adjective to describe the movie in lines 5 and 6. Today, OK is like a blank canvas that, with a change of voice or context, can take on different meanings. But it wasn't always that way; over the past 200 years, OK has grown a lot, taking on roles that are purely functional (managing conversation flow) in addition to adding meanings like "approved." The story of how it got those roles tells us just as much about ourselves as it does about OK.

Of course, the ability to have different meanings in different contexts is not unique to OK—lots of words are versatile like that.[2] But OK is special because the events that shaped it and created those meanings are still visible in its functions and spellings (i.e., OK, okay, oke doke, and kk). OK is young for a word—less than 200 years old—so the inventions and cultural revolutions it has witnessed are mostly documented. And OK has been at the center of all of them. Every major technological change since the steam-powered rotary printing press of the 1830s to the spread of video calls in the 2020s has helped to shape OK.

Agreement OK (the one that means "all correct") started with the steam-powered rotary printing press (Chapter 2), and approval OK (the one that can be a noun, e.g. "I need to

---

[2]Take "so" for example. Just like OK, so can be an interjection, "so, when are we getting ice cream?"; it can also be a conjunction, "I was hot, so I ate ice cream"; and an intensifier, "it was so hot." The intensifier type of so is another great example of language change. Intensifier so has been able to modify adjectives for a long time, but so to modify other things is new. It's so new that only some people accept it as correct. For example, "I am so going to get ice cream today" is only accepted by a portion of native English speakers.

get your OK on this") comes out of the railroads (Chapter 4). The formal spelling of okay was a literary invention and a response to high-brow and low-brow language, a cultural force that was exacerbated by late nineteenth century publishing (Chapter 5). Discourse marker OK (the one that keeps a conversation going or changes the subject) is tied to the telephone (Chapter 6) while oke doke (also okey dokey, etc.) comes out of the electrification of urban America and corresponding cultural upheaval of the 1920s (also Chapter 6). The globalization of OK stems from televisions and the Cold War (Chapter 7) and K (and other abbreviations of abbreviations) is an artifact of the internet (Chapter 8). Finally, the nearly infinite creative adaptations of OK (i.e., kk, okieee, okie-dokeee, etc.) emerged in response to the rise of social media (Chapter 9).

Each of these meanings, uses, and shapes tell a story about OK, but they also tell a story about the relationship between language and technology. OK's youth may be deceiving because it has lived a full life and has become symbolic of the ways that language and technologies interact. The many shapes of OK (ok, OK, okay, okey dokey, etc.) each contain a story about a time and a place. Collectively, those stories expose the ways that language is shaped by technology, and vice versa.

But you and I are not the first to notice that OK is special, and this isn't even the first book about OK. There are three research papers and one book (at least) that focus solely on OK. The papers were all written by Allen Walker Read, and the book was written by Allan Metcalf. Read is the reason we know about OK: he uncovered that first instance and tied it directly to the language play of the 1830s. He documented its urban legend and folklore and uncovered series of events that led from its invention to its popularity by tracing its role in the 1840 presidential election. Metcalf situates OK in the larger American identity and demonstrates how OK is emblematic of an American philosophy.

The present book is built on the foundation laid by the others but takes a different approach by focusing our attention on what OK teaches us about the relationship between language and technology. Exploring the details of OK—it's shapes and functions as well as its myths and origins—illustrates how language and technology shape each other. And more than any other word, OK exemplifies how technology is written into language.

Language change happens with or without writing or other technologies—it is a natural part of human language evolution. But, since the invention of writing, the fate of every language has been intertwined with communication technologies. With every new medium (writing, printing, telephones, the internet, etc.), the norms and expectations for communication change, thereby changing the language. Since we use language every day, any change can be hard to see. But, with OK, the traces of language change are clearly visible in its meanings and spellings. Those traces have come to define OK and catapult it into becoming the most popular word in the world.

2 OLL KORRECT (ORIGINS)

The origins of OK would likely still be shrouded in mystery and urban legend if it weren't for Allen Walker Read. Read was a professor at Columbia University and scholar of American English. Read read extensively and spent his career uncovering the origins of some of English's most powerful and elusive words such as OK. In 1963 and 1964, Read published a series of articles in *American Speech* that proved definitively that OK began as a bit of language play in the mid-nineteenth century. His discovery did not stop the proliferation of urban legends about OK, but he did offer a concrete and defensible origin for it.

Read discovered OK in the response to a letter to the editor in the March 23rd, 1839 issue of the *Boston Morning Post*. In it, the *Boston Morning Post* editor, Charles Gorden Greene (who was always very witty), is responding to a letter from the Providence Journal editor.[1]

---

[1] Read, "The First Stage in the History of 'O. K.,'" pg 12

The above is from the Providence Journal, the editor of which is a little too quick on the trigger, on this occasion. We said not a word about our deputation passing "through the city" of Providence. We said our brethren were going to New York in the Richmond, and they did go, as per Post of Thursday. The "Chairman of the Committee on Charity Lecture Bells" [Thomas B. Fearing], is one of the deputation, and perhaps if he should return to Boston, via Providence, he of the [Providence] Journal, and his train-band, would have the "contribution box," et ceteras, o.k— all correct—and cause the corks to fly, like sparks, upward.

That's it—the first instance of OK—an acronym for all correct. While according to all normal conventions, "all correct" should be shortened as *a.c.,* not *o.k.,* this kind of creative respelling was popular in 1830s Boston, and not limited to *o.k.,* so surely didn't strike readers as being out of the ordinary.

From the late 1830s through the early 1840s, acronyms were everywhere in what seems to have been an explosion in linguistic creativity. Newspapers in East Coast cities (Boston, New York City, Philadelphia) regularly incorporated acronyms into their articles, substituting *O. F. M.* for Our First Men (a fashionable phrase of the time), and *n. g.* for no go.[2] But this linguistic creativity wasn't confined to newspapers; accounts of the time suggest that people used acronyms for everything from

---

[2]Ibid.

ordering drinks at the bar (*w. b.* for wine bitters) to referring to stores (*o. b. s.* for Old Boston Stone, where one could get ice cream). It was linguistic mania! And it was also a completely natural response to changing communication media.

This moment in East Coast newspapers is emblematic of the relationship between language and technology, illustrating how people play with language when presented with new media.[3] The early 1830s was all about the Penny Press. Penny Presses were daily newspapers that were both cheap (1-2 cents per issue) and widely distributed. Though Benjamin Day's 1932 establishment of the *Boston Sun* is widely considered to be the precipitating event that launched them, there is more context. The story of the Penny Press is one of radical new inventions, society's evolving relationship with literacy, and how markets shape the world.

The Penny Press

The Penny Press was made possible by a combination of technology (the steam-powered cylindrical press), a culture of literacy, and the American market economy. Each of these forces directly contributed to the invention of the Penny

---

[3]Marshall McLuhan takes this idea a step further with his idea that "the medium is the message" (Understanding Media: The Extensions of Man, 1964).

Press and correspondingly, the moment of widespread linguistic creativity that gave us OK.

From 1830 to 1840, there was a 10-fold increase in the number of newspapers in the United States. In 1830 there were just over 300 and by 1840, there were 3,267.[4] Before 1830, newspapers were almost exclusively aimed at the wealthiest members of society. They were high-brow publications intended for readers who could afford them. Since printing was expensive, newspaper owners made a profit by selling a few papers at a high markup. In the 1830's, the last piece of the puzzle was put into place that radically changed this model and made printing cheap enough to sell to the masses with only a small markup, and the start of the Penny Press. It was transformational but required three things to be in place: the technology, literacy, and a free market.

The Penny Press was made technically possible because of an improvement to the printing press. In the early 1800's, Friedrich Gottlob Koenig realized that cylinders could be used to create a faster printing press for dual-sided printing. He took this idea to the center of industrialization: London. There, he (and a talented watchmaker, Andreas Friedrich Bauer) built the first steam-powered cylindrical press in 1804. Traditional machines printed 200-300 pages an hour; the Koenig-Bauer press could print over 1,100.

---

[4]"Chronicling America Temporal Coverage (Entire Collection) - Chronicling America: Historic American Newspapers | Tableau Public."

In 1814, they found their first client: *The Times* of London. By buying the press, *The Times* was treading into volatile territory. The political climate of 1814 London was tense—factories were filled with distrust and anger over technology replacing laborer's jobs and it was spilling into the street. The owners of *The Times* were concerned that their printing staff—like the Luddites—would try to destroy the new technology.[5] So, to avoid confrontation, they built new presses and printed the first issue in secret. On the morning of November 29th, 1814, readers read the first paper printed with the new technology. Aside from *The Times*' own announcement, no one could tell the difference.

> Our Journal of this day presents to the public the practical result of the greatest improvement connected with printing, since the discovery of the art itself. The reader of this paragraph now holds in his hand, one of the many thousand impressions of *The Times* newspaper, which were taken off last night by a mechanical apparatus. A system of machinery almost organic has been devised and arranged, which, while it relieves the human frame of its most laborious efforts in printing, far exceeds all human powers in rapidity and dispatch . . .

---

[5]The Luddites were textile manufacturers in the early nineteenth century who opposed technology and machinery that could make their jobs obsolete. They regularly destroyed equipment that they felt was a threat.

Of course, Koenig and Bauer were not the only ones working on improving printing efficiency. As early as 1784, French printers were experimenting with cylinders for printing books, too. So even though Koenig and Bauer contributed the breakthrough idea, the need for better, faster printing was felt by all. That need was driven by increasingly high literacy levels and a society that wanted reading materials.

By the eighteenth century, literacy was spreading across Europe. Both John Locke and Jean-Jacques Rousseau had been influential in the establishment of schools, and both advocated for education across economic strata (not just for the wealthy). As more people learned to read, there was more demand for printed materials—any printed materials. For most people, books were too expensive to purchase (even used), but they could afford more ephemeral media like newspapers and pamphlets.

As Europe became increasingly urbanized, it became feasible to distribute periodicals throughout the cities and surrounding areas. In eighteenth century England, this meant a steady increase in the number of (relatively expensive) newspapers and a still-growing demand for print. So, by the time Koenig arrived in 1804, London was a hotbed of activity for journalism and printing technology.[6]

---

[6]Feather, *A History of British Publishing*

Widespread literacy wasn't limited to Europe; it was central to American culture, too. Many of the American colonists were Puritans, and Puritans believed that everyone needed to read the Bible for themselves ("everyone" included both enslaved persons and females).[7] So, they established schools and encouraged everyone to learn to read. In the American context, this religious significance helped push literacy levels beyond European levels by the early nineteenth century.[8]

Like their European counterparts, literate Americans demanded reading material. However, demand alone did not inspire the Penny Press—it required the right economic context, too. The American economy was controlled by the British until the late 1780s, so local demand didn't matter because everything was based on trade. However, the American Revolution gave way to the American market economy, and in a market, demand matters. In a market, businesspeople can decide how they want to make a profit: sell a few things with a big margin or a lot of things with a small margin.[9] Though for Penny Presses to make sense, they still needed better printing technology, this economic context helps explain why they were an American (rather than British) invention.[10]

---

[7]Cohen, "The School upon a Hill."
[8]Cohen.
[9]Harper, "Mercantilism and the American Revolution."
[10]Nerone, "The Mythology of the Penny Press."

Making a Linguistic Community

Once cheap papers became available, everyone started reading all of the time, and by the late 1830s, most Americans had access to reading material. In fact, there were so many readers that editors could differentiate their audiences. One paper might be targeted to high-brow readers, another to low-brow. There were political papers, social ones, and fiction.

This differentiation influenced the linguistic choices editors made. Aside from the topics covered in the paper (i.e., politics, fashion, farming, etc.), the best way to signal who a paper was for was with the kind of language it used. There's the obvious choice of vocabulary and sentence structure, but there's also the less obvious process of creating an "in-group" language. It's this in-group language that led to the invention of OK.

The *Boston Morning Post* (OK's birthplace) was a Democratic paper that targeted a working-class audience. It ran every day except Sunday and was filled with the morning's news, political commentary, editorial discussion, and other topics of local interest. Typical of the time, readers of the *Boston Morning Post* were mostly active, devoted readers. Being a *Boston Morning Post* reader would have been a part of one's identity and if they spoke to another *Post* reader, they would have a lot in common.

They would share politics and the language to talk about it. They would know the same abbreviations and would use them in the same ways. (By contrast, a Whig party paper would have different conventions). Though all these papers were written in (American) English, they had slight variations that reflected the tone. For example, *O. F. M.* stood for "our first men" (locally important people) and being a Democrat or a Whig determined if that phrase was being used sarcastically or in earnest. Likewise, daily readers of any paper would be keeping up with newly invented abbreviations. So, when *O. F. M.* (or *o. k.*) showed up again, there was no need to provide the translation since it was provided the day (or week) before.

Because many papers established these hyper-local conventions, not everyone would or could just pick up a paper and understand the subtext: to read the *Boston Morning Post*, one had to already be a reader. This tight readership created a linguistic community, and linguistic communities can do all kinds of interesting things with language because they evolve together. So, after it was coined, when a journalist wrote *o. k.* as an acronym for "all correct," readers had the context to interpret the social commentary. Unfortunately for us, the specific commentary has been lost to the passage of time. However, we have some clues.

First, the intentional misspelling of "all correct" as "oll korrect" was probably a play on phonetics. Phonetic misspellings are often used to represent speech, and especially dialects or idiosyncrasies of non-standard speech. This technique is regularly used in fiction to represent characters, but when it appears in non-fiction, the intended connotation is often poking fun at best and derogatory at worst. When

Greene misspelled all correct as "oll korrect," he was likely trying to slight the *Providence Journal's* 24-year-old editor, Henry Anthony. Given that Boston was bigger than Providence, it could have been meant to call him provincial or simply uneducated. The jump from the misspelling to the acronym is a short one since there are almost no rules for how acronyms and abbreviations get made.

Second, acronyms were all the rage in the late 1830's Northeast: a young man might have gone to the bar and said something like "gimme a w.b. [wine bitters] and a p.w.s [port wine sangaree]." To which the bartender might have replied "a.r. [all right], coming right up!".[11] It was fun, it was flirty, and the cultural pervasiveness was typical during a time of accelerated language change.

Acronyms, abbreviations, and slang all subtly communicate ownership over a language. Adolescents of every generation invent these terms to some extent, creating new words and repurposing old ones. This is such a well-established part of communication that some words become part of the generational identity (i.e., rad, boss, daddy-o, or even bae). Newspapers did more than spread information: they spread access to written language. This access radically changed who owned the language. It was a democratization

---

[11] Wine bitters and iced brandy punch must have been popular drinks as they were both referenced in the *Boston Morning Sun* in 1838/39. Read, "The First Stage in the History of 'O. K.'"

of print—more people were writing and reading than ever before and publishing was moving out of the hands of a few into the hands of many.

This normal process of linguistic innovation is amplified during times of technological change (such as with the advent of the Penny Press, or the emergence of digital technology and smartphones).[12] During these periods, words and phrases are invented as people push the boundaries of their new communication tools. From 1830 to 1840 in both the United States and England, journalists played with linguistic conventions, inventing countless abbreviations and acronyms. But only OK remains.

When it was invented, *o. k.* was part of a class of misspelled playful acronyms including *k. g.* for "no go" or "no good" (kno go/ kno good), and *k. y.* for "no use" (kno yuse). Though the origins of *k. g.* and *k. y.* are still a mystery, there are at least two possibilities for why these misspellings were in circulation. The first is the same as OK—it was poking fun at an unnamed person's dialect or editorial quality. The second is that they are referencing then-president Andrew Jackson. Jackson was a notoriously bad speller, and is quoted as saying "it is a damn poor mind that can think of only one way to spell a word"; it is now understood that he probably had dyslexia, but at the time, he was just a part of his identity.[13]

---

[12]McSweeney, *The Pragmatics of Text Messaging.*
[13]Read, "Could Andrew Jackson Spell?"

Jackson was also highly contentious: people either loved him or hated him. So, *k. y.* and *k. g.* could have been endearing recreations of Jacksonian-spelling by Democrats or mocking his shortcomings by Whigs (or both).

O.k. was also in competition with two acronyms that had a similar meaning: *a. r.* for all right, and *o. w.* for all right. Though there is no evidence of *a. c.* for all correct, the presence of *a. r.* and *o. w.* (and absence of *a. c.*) suggest a trajectory for OK that highlights its playful origins.[14]

A. r. probably came first given that it is the most literal acronymization. *O. w.* may have been a play on *a .r.* (again it could have been poking fun at a dialect or referencing Jackson, we may never know). Once *o. w.* was being thrown about as an acronym for two misspelled words, newspaper readers were primed to tolerate acronyms of even misspelled words. By 1838 (just months before *o. k.*'s debut), *o. w.* was being thrown about for "all right" and appearing in multiple newspapers without explanation.[15]

By the end of 1839, most of the working-class East Coast papers had made the switch and were using acronyms liberally. As with all language change, even though one media may drive the change, it will spread across communication modalities. For example, the New York *Evening Tattler* both used these abbreviations and commented on them:

---

[14]Read, "The First Stage in the History of 'O. K.'"
[15]Ibid.

A paper, printed on half-a-sheet, somewhere near the verge of creation in Illinois, requests us to exchange. K. G. (No go.)[16]

A paper in Indiana inquires of us why we will not exchange. Answer K.Y. (no use.)[17]

The editors explicitly mention that this form of language play was not only widespread but also primarily a spoken phenomenon:

THE INITIAL LANGUAGE. This is a species of spoken short-hand, which is getting into very general use among loafers and gentlemen of the fancy [. . .].[18]

Less than 6 weeks later, the editors themselves adopted OK in print:

These "wise men from the East," who came so far to enlighten our darkness, are right enough, of course, to play at bowls with us as long as we are willing to set ourselves up, like skittles, to be knocked down for their amusement and emolument. OK ! all correct![19]

---

[16]New York *Evening Tattler*, July 26, 1839, p. 2/2.
[17]New York *Evening Tattler*, August 5, 1839, P. 2/2.
[18]New York *Evening Tattler*, July 27, 1839, p. 2/2.
[19]New York *Evening Tattler*, September 2, 1839, p. 2/2.

OK was not limited to just a few papers, but appeared—along with other acronyms—across the East Coast. Some editors even wrote articles covering the rise of this "Initial Language" and how initials were fashionable in both speaking and writing.[20] But fashions are temporary, and in the same way that people get tired of songs, clothes, and other trends, they grew tired of slang, too. By the mid 1840s, most editors banned their journalists from using non-standardized acronyms and abbreviations, spelling the end of language play in mainstream newspapers.

But how did OK slip past? For that, we need to revisit the presidential election of 1840, when the Whig party candidate, William Henry Harrison, defeated Democratic incumbent Martin Van Buren.

---

[20]Similar to articles and books written at the beginning of the 21st Century about "Netspeak" and "Computer Mediated Communication."

3 OK? (ALTERNATIVE ORIGINS)

Before we get started with the role OK played in politics, we first need to address some rumors. OK's humble beginnings may have seemed—to some—too humble. While Allan Walker Read established that OK is the remaining relic of a period of linguistic play sweeping Boston, many other creation myths abound.[1] Now we will turn to H. L. Mencken, a renowned lexicographer who compiled OK's creation myths while writing his 1919 treatise on American English.[2] But Mencken and Read were not the last people to be fascinated with the history of OK. Another linguist-historian, Allan Metcalf, in his retrospective on OK, collected even more myths to explain its birth. While all these origin stories have been debunked, they tell us about ourselves, and our

---

[1]We can imagine another book years from now about LOL and how it was born of the digital age but had much earlier roots.

[2]Mencken, *American Language*; Mencken, *The American Language Supplement 1*.

tendency to explain our world in a way that gives ourselves (and our language) slightly better beginnings.

Grains of Truth

When the world seems incomplete, we, as humans, often want to fill in the details. This first group of stories all hold some grain of truth about OK's origins, but the details are simply wrong.

We'll begin with my own. As a child, I personally believed that OK stood for Olde Kinderhook, a Boston journalist who signed all his columns O.K. In this version, Olde Kinderhook was so popular that when a new journalist took over his column, he just kept using O.K.'s initials. I was not completely wrong (O.K. did stand for Olde Kinderhook), but I was not right (Olde Kinderhook was a nickname for former U.S. president Martin Van Buren, not a journalist).

But I wasn't the only one confused about who was behind OK. In the 1920s, a lot of people believed that OK was invented by former President Andrew Jackson.[3] There are multiple versions of this myth, but the most prominent is that he misspelled "all correct" in a memo. After the typo, the abbreviation was adopted with pride by his supporters

---

[3]Read, "The Folklore of 'O. K.'"; Metcalf, *OK*; Mencken, *The American Language Supplement 1*.

and derision by his detractors. There is no record of this misspelling, but Jackson was tangentially involved in the Old Kinderhook part of OK's history, so there is a small connection there.

Another Jacksonian origin is that OK is a misspelling of the abbreviation for Ordered Record (a type of legal document) that appeared in a memo from Jackson inquiring about the details of a sale of a person who had been enslaved. Again, Jackson was a major American cultural figure at the time of OK's birth, but there are a few problems with this myth. *O.R.* was a common abbreviation for Ordered Record, and the correct abbreviation appears two times in this same document. There is no reason to think that Jackson would have substituted a 'K' for an 'R' because he was a poor speller given that K/R is an uncommon—even unheard of—substitution. However, these two letters look a lot alike, and further examination of the document in question suggests that Jackson may have had poor penmanship.[4]

Ultimately, the myths in this group are like the Japanese art of kintsugi, where broken pottery is repaired with gold. In these myths, the bits of truth are held together with interesting details, giving OK a more refined origin than it had before. But that isn't the only type of myth we make: sometimes a happy coincidence gets misinterpreted as an origin.

---

[4] Read, "The Folklore of 'O. K.'"

An Exotic Loanword

Human language is fascinating because it is both infinite and finite. It is infinite because we can always say new things or invent new words, but it is finite because there are only so many sounds we can produce.[5] This fact results in language overlap. Sounds that exist in one language are likely to exist in another, resulting in happy coincidences of similar words across languages.[6] This has led some to posit that OK is a case of borrowing from another language. The most widely referenced instance is borrowing from Choctaw, but there is also Wolof, Scottish, and French (via Haiti), among others. These exotic tales try to imbue OK with more depth while writing off the realities of nineteenth century racism.

The most prominent of the exotic loanword myths is that OK derives from the Choctaw word *okeh* which means "it is" or "it is so." Choctaw is spoken by members of the Choctaw tribe who lived in the area that is now Mississippi. When Colonists arrived in Mississippi around 1830, Choctaws were forcibly relocated along with other American Indian tribes in an event known as the Trail of Tears. In one version of this myth (the one recovered by our linguist-historian, Allan

---

[5]Signed languages are just as limited by this reality and similar handshapes appear across different languages.
[6]In addition, lots of languages have common ancestors, resulting in even more overlap.

Metcalf), Andrew Jackson is again the star. As the myth goes, Jackson is painted in a favorable light, completely out of sync with the social dynamics of the day. It is said that while negotiating treaties with the Choctaw leadership, he became enamored with Choctaw and started saying *okeh*.

This myth gained a lot of traction and was even endorsed by former U.S. president Woodrow Wilson. During the late nineteenth century, *okeh* appeared as a trade name for a variety of items from collars to phonographs, and there was even a British condiment, O.K. Sauce, that included this myth on the label.[7]

However, it is unlikely that OK was borrowed from Choctaw. First, Choctaws were persecuted by European Americans. While dominant groups often engage in cultural appropriation of persecuted groups, borrowing a single word and no other cultural artifacts is virtually unheard of. Second, though there was a significant missionary presence in Choctaw communities at this time, contact with English speakers was otherwise limited.[8] Any contact would have been mediated by English—not Choctaw—since English was the dominant language. As a result, English speakers had very little exposure to *okeh*, certainly not enough for transfer to occur (even if Jackson used it first).

---

[7] Read, "The Folklore of 'O. K.'"; Metcalf, OK.
[8] https://www.choctawnation.com/

Finally, *okeh* is a function word (it is syntactically necessary, but semantically meaningless), and function words are rarely borrowed. Function words include prepositions (at, in, on), determiners (the, this, a), auxiliary verbs (to be), and other words that do more for grammar than meaning. *Okeh* is like the auxiliary verb, to be. So, the Choctaw myth essentially says that *okeh*, the auxiliary verb, turned into OK, all correct. There is no other recorded instance of a language's function word becoming another language's content word. This myth is simply unrealistic. Trying to ascribe OK to Choctaw ignores the social realities of how language change happens and tries to rewrite the depth of persecution experienced by Choctaws. But Choctaw isn't the only language entangled in this process.

In 1969, David Dalby, an African languages scholar, found two quotes from enslaved persons both dating the mid-1700's that he linked to modern-day OK. He used these to argue that OK came from a West African language such as Wolof or Mande:

Kay, massa, you just leave me, me sit here, great fish jump up into da canoe, here he be, massa, fine fish, massa.

Oh ki, massa, doctor no need be fright, we no want to hurt him.[9]

---

[9]Dalby, "O.K., A.O.K. and O KE."

The first quote is trusted as an accurate recording. The second is not.[10] The second quotation should be written "Oh, ki", not "Oh ki." In Wolof, *kay* means come, but it's also an all-purpose interjection, similar to "come on" or "come now." In many languages in the Mande family, *oh, ki* roughly translates to "that's it" or "certainly." Neither one of these quotations demonstrates that OK was a widely used expression among enslaved persons except to say that these words do exist. Secondly, this myth has all the same problems as the Choctaw myth: there is no reason to think that a function word would be borrowed or that a dominant group would borrow an interjection from a marginalized one. Like the Choctaw myth, this one repaints the past in a more harmonious light. Unlike the Choctaw myth, this one demonstrates how a single quotation can be wound into an entire story.

Sonorous Coincidences

Choctaw and Wolof/Mande are the most widespread examples of a whole collection of myths that link OK to other languages. Many of these myths are proposed by English speakers who spot the connection in another language. For example, a journalist with the London *Observer* noticed that

---

[10]Cassidy, "OK. Is It African?"

Scots English *Och aye* sounded a lot like the American English OK, and *och aye* means "oh, yes."[11] The journalist proposed that since many Scots emigrated to the United States (though he had never been himself), OK must be borrowed from Scots English. Though the connection is purely speculation, it was widely accepted at the time. The biggest problem is that the timeline is wrong: Scottish migration began in the 1700s and OK appeared 100 years later. But the invention of a Scottish origin for OK illustrates our proclivity to transform coincidences into explanations.

Similarly, there is a story that OK derives from the Haitian port of Aux Cayes, which imported a popular rum. In this myth, the rum was so good that its port of origin was shorthand for the rum, and the rum became shorthand for anything good. Only problem is the rum might not have been so good.

There is also the Greek expression, *Olla Kalla* (Όλα Κάλλα), which does mean something like OK. However, there is no evidence for enough contact between Greek speakers and American English speakers in the early or mid-nineteenth century to warrant the transfer.[12] But it is nice that "all correct" is an expression in Greek, too.

---

[11]Mencken, *American Language*; Mencken, *The American Language Supplement 1*.

[12]Mencken, *The American Language Supplement 1*; Read, "The Folklore of 'O. K.'"

There are many myths of this sort, tracing the origins of OK to German, French, Finnish, and Latin, but none of them are accurate.[13] They are all either inventions like the Choctaw myth or happy coincidences like the Greek myth. Often, if we look hard enough, we can find similarities anywhere, but that effect isn't just limited to language—even food has inspired OK, too.

Food

When the American Civil War began, there was an immediate need for large quantities of portable food, and biscuits are a perfect solution. So, O. Kendall—a biscuit maker in Chicago—started baking, stamping the initials of his bakery into the top of each biscuit. Apparently, these biscuits were better than other army rations, so—as the story goes—soldiers started referring to everything good as OK.[14] There's only one problem: The Civil War began in 1861; OK was already in use by 1839.

There is another baker myth that traces OK to vanilla cookies in a Boston bakery. This time the baker's name was Otto Kimmel, but it's the same idea: he made tasty cookies

---

[13]Read, "The Folklore of 'O. K.'"; Metcalf, *OK*; Mencken, *American Language*.
[14]Mencken, *The American Language Supplement 1*; Read, "The Folklore of 'O. K.'"; Metcalf, *OK*.

and stamped his initials into them.[15] There's also delicious apples from Kinderhook, NY, where the crates came stamped with the initials, O.K. (though it's unclear what the O stood for).[16]

The common thread across all of OK's food origin myths is that the foods were beloved. Each of these myths instills a nearly visceral relationship between an exceptional food and an exceptional word. Maybe by drawing the connection between beloved foods, we can imagine an OK that is more than just OK, but was invented from a place of love and respect.

In the end, these myths tell us about ourselves, and how we explain our language. Language is an incredible human feat, so incredible that it inspires its users to explain where it came from. But OK doesn't need any help—it's true origin and evolution is a fantastic tale, full of political intrigue, social connection, and transformational inventions that have not only shaped language, but the very fabric of communication.

---

[15]Metcalf, *OK*.
[16]Ibid.

4 OLDE KINDERHOOK (BRANDING)

The presidential election of 1840 was heated. The United States was on the brink of financial disaster, populism was on the rise, and the sitting president, Martin Van Buren, was viewed as pretentious and uncaring. Newly establish Penny Presses were bringing the drama into everyone's homes. OK sat at the center of it all: at the beginning of 1840, it was in its infancy, a regional expression for "all correct." But, when the Democrats took it up as part of their campaign strategy, it quickly spread across the United States. And by the time William Henry Harrison was sworn in as the ninth U.S. President, everyone had heard of OK.

The drama of the 1840 election began in 1836. 1836 was the end of Andrew Jackson's second term as president and Democrats felt he should be replaced. Jackson's vice president, Martin Van Buren, was nominated to represent the Democratic party, and William Henry Harrison was picked to represent the Whigs (no Republicans yet). In 1836, Van Buren easily won, and the Whigs learned a lot about how to work with the media. So, in 1840, the Whigs had become politically savvy and leveraged the Penny Press to maximum effect.

It was a smear campaign. It was Democrat Van Buren versus Whig Harrison again. It started with the Whigs calling Van Buren a "Kinderhook cabbage planter" (he was born in Kinderhook, New York) and Democrats calling the Whigs "silk stockings" (because they were perceived as wealthy and out of touch). Both parties took it in stride, turning the insults into slogans. But Democrats stumbled badly when they established Old Hickory Clubs for Democrats to convene. It would have been fine, except Old Hickory was Jackson's nickname and Jackson wasn't running—Van Buren was. The Whigs used this to maximum effect, asking if the race was between Old Hickory, and Old Tip (Harrison's nickname after winning a battle at Tippecanoe). The Democrats quickly changed the club names from Old Hickory to O.K.—without explanation. They were trying to coin a new nickname for Van Buren, Old Kinderhook, while simultaneously referencing OK's more familiar meaning as an acronym for all correct.[1] As noted in the *Tammany Newspaper* in March of 1840:

THE DEMOCRATIC O.K. CLUB, are hereby ordered to meet at the House of Jacob Colvin, 245 Grand Street, on Tuesday evening . . . [2]

---

[1]Read, "The Second Stage in the History of 'O. K.'"
[2]*Tammany Newspaper*, March 27, 1840, p. 3/2. Ibid p. 84.

O.K. took off, and O.K. Clubs spread across the country, but Democrats didn't explain their thinking until two months later, when they finally said that Old Kinderhook was the Democratic answer to Old Tip:

> JACKSON BREAST PIN. We acknowledge the receipt of a very pretty gold Pin . . . and having upon it the (to the "Whigs") very frightful letters O.K., significant of the birthplace of Martin Van Buren, old Kinderhook, as also the rallying word of the Democracy of the late election, "all correct." It can be purchased at Mr. P. L. Fierty's, 486 Pearl Street. Those who wear them should bear in mind that it will require their most strenuous exertions between this and autumn to make all things O.K.[3]

The pun made it a perfect slogan. No longer confined to the East Coast, Democrats pushed OK across the country. Recognizing the slogan meant being clued into the politics of the time, and something larger than oneself; recognizing the pin on someone else's lapel meant recognizing a friend (or a foe).

The slogan was successful: Democrats and Whigs both adopted it. Democrats called themselves "the O.K. fraternity," and Whigs were quite satisfied to have a clear label for this rowdy group. Being part of the Tammany Hall machine, the O.K.s were not only in favor of Democracy, but also not afraid to cause a scene. At one event, they infiltrated a Whig

---

[3]New York *New Era*, May 27, 1840, p. 2/6. Ibid p. 86.

procession with their own flag bearing the letters O.K. At another, they started a riot at a Whig event, attracting media attention all the way.[4] The Whigs did their part to spread the word, playing with the phrase by calling the O.K.s the K.O.s for "kicked out and kicked over." They even created alternative meanings for O.K.: after winning an election in Connecticut, they boasted, "Last and most approved version—O.K. OLD KONNECTICUT!!!"[5] More alternative meanings included but weren't limited to "O.K., i.e. 'Ole Korrect', Out of 'Kash', Out of 'Kredit', Out of 'Karacter', and Out of 'Klothes.'"[6]

But a good slogan isn't enough to win an election, and Van Buren lost. OK, however, became lexicalized and established itself in American English. For the most part, it was used to communicate that something was "all correct," but context is key, and—as with all political symbols—for a subset of the population and for a period of time, it could be read as opposition to the Whigs.

OK Products

OK as a political slogan is just a type of branding—constructing an image to sell to the public. It should come

---

[4]Read, "The Second Stage in the History of 'O. K.'"
[5]New York *Times*, April 13, 1840, p. 1/2. Ibid, p. 97.
[6]New York *Daily Express*, April 24, 1840, p. 1/2. Ibid, p. 97.

as no surprise then that OK has been used to sell cola, magazines, toys, and more.

OK as a brand name has a certain appeal to advertisers: it's international, it's short, and it's easy to say. The problem is that OK is not necessarily good, nor is it descriptive. Take the case of OK Soda. In 1993, the Coca-Cola Company decided that OK would be an excellent way to market soda. The style was dark: neo-noir imagery with disconcertingly negative advertisements. Many of the cans featured expressionless faces in gray scale stamped with OK in block letters. The marketing slogan was, "Things are going to be OK," and the vision was to sell a feeling rather than taste. But OK is not a particularly good feeling and wasn't good enough to sell the soda. After testing it in a selection of American cities, Coca-Cola decided that the product was not viable and pulled it from shelves in 1995, before it went into national— or international—circulation.

Why did Coca-Cola's marketing team think that OK Soda would be a success? In the late 1980s, Coca-Cola commissioned an international study on word and brand recognition and found that "Coke" was the fourth most recognizable word in the world.[7] The first most recognizable word? OK. Thus, OK Soda was conceived. The problem was that no one understood what they were being sold or why, illustrating that recognition and clarity are not synonymous.

---

[7]McGregor, Symonds, and Foust, "How Failure Breeds Success."

But OK itself wasn't doomed: it could, as it would turn out, sell a magazine. The same year that OK Soda was flopping in the United States, *OK! Magazine* was establishing itself in the United Kingdom. Launched in April 1993, *OK! Magazine* is the largest international lifestyle magazine and is consistently ranked in the top 200 magazines in each market. So why can OK sell gossip but not soda?

First, there's a slight distinction in the orthography: *OK! Magazine* is not just OK, it's OK! With the exclamation point, OK becomes enthusiastic and any passive reading is made unavailable. Orthography is key for how we reconcile ambiguity, but there are other strategies, too. There is imagery: OK Soda's color palette was intentionally severe, signifying the less than great interpretation of OK, whereas *OK!*'s imagery is colorful photos of celebrities. OK Soda's marketing campaign communicated a resignation to the state of the world being no better than OK, while *OK!* communicates excitement for the lives of others.

There are more distinctions to be made, but the interesting bit is that in the same year, two different companies saw an opportunity in OK and used it in their branding. And while 1993 was a banner year for OK, other companies have seen this same opportunity, using OK to sell everything from toys (OK! Dolls) and apps (OK Play) to poultry (O.K. Foods). Each of these companies tried to leverage the universal nature of OK to sell products. The assumption in every case is that since OK is a nearly universal word, labeling a product OK would make it recognizable.

Today, when companies use OK in their branding, they are drawing on the foundations established in the 1840 presidential campaign to push OK into national attention. But OK's popularity in the United States doesn't explain its global adoption. For that, we will have to go deeper into the relationship between OK and technology.

5 OKAY (LITERATURE)

Though OK was born written, it would be more than 30 years old before any well-known author would even try to slip it into a book. There are two documented instances of mainstream authors trying to use OK.[1] The first was by Henry David Thoreau and the second by Louisa May Alcott.[2] Both were unafraid to push boundaries in their writing, so why didn't they defend their use of OK? Just as curiously, why didn't their contemporaries like Walt Whitman and Mark Twain (both known for unconventional writing) use it? The answers lie in the relationship between literacy, culture, and technology.

Americans in the nineteenth century were overwhelmingly literate. Literacy rates were the highest

---

[1] It was used by less popular and more vulgar authors throughout the nineteenth century, but even then, only the most illiterate and crass characters dared utter it.

[2] Metcalf, "OK." Thoreau and Alcott were not mainstream, but they were both well respected authors, and their work was published by mainstream publishing houses.

in cities, but even in rural areas, upwards of 75% of the total population could read, and many cities reached 99% literacy by 1840.[3] Even women learned to read because to be good wives and mothers, they needed to pass literacy on to their children.[4] Furthermore, colonists and early Americans relied more heavily on print media for news, entertainment, and gossip than we do even today. Before telephone and radio were invented, people could either talk to each other or read, so they read—a lot.

By the time steam-powered printing and cheap paper were invented in the early nineteenth century, there was an eager market for fast, cheap reading material. Newspapers were the perfect medium. Penny Presses swept the United States, and nearly every demographic had a paper just for them. Not only the Democrats and the Whigs, but every church had a newspaper, and every activist group, too. They were also accessible to all classes of people, so even poor Americans and immigrants could afford reading material.[5]

But poor people wanted novels, too, and couldn't possibly afford to buy new books. Even though paperbacks had become much cheaper (with mechanically made paper and a

---

[3]Grubb, "Growth of Literacy in Colonial America."

[4]There is speculation that early Americans had overall higher literacy levels than Americans today because linguistically dense texts were widely read (such as Thomas Paine's *Common Sense*). Mahajan, "Were Colonial Americans More Literate than Americans Today?"

[5]King, "'Literature of the Kitchen.'"

switch from leather binding to canvas), a single book could still cost 2 weeks of a teacher's salary or a more than a month of a servant's. Even secondhand books were too expensive for most servants (and they didn't make publishers any money). A few savvy businessmen saw this as an opportunity and started distributing serialized novels and books in newspaper format. First they republished out of print materials, but quickly turned to foreign novels. Because of a loophole in copyright laws, when a new book arrived from Europe, it could be reprinted in the United States without paying any royalties. Though this loophole was closed by the end of the 1850s, it still had a transformational effect on publishing.[6]

Turnaround time on a pirated novel was quick: by some accounts, a new novel could come into the port in the morning and be sold on the streets that evening. This business model had two effects that were important for OK. First, serialized novels became accessible and with that, class distinctions in literature became even more important. Second, especially when the copyright restrictions were tightened, publishers ran out of content and had to turn to domestic authors, sparking the beginning of American literature.

The class distinctions had always been present in publishing, but since lower classes couldn't afford books at all, those distinctions weren't codified into literature until

---

[6]Gross and Cohen, "Building a National Literature"; King, "'Literature of the Kitchen.'"

novels-as-newspapers emerged to meet lower class demand. These cheap serial novels did not have the cultural capital of a book—they were ephemeral, intended to be read and discarded. Cheap works were also strictly intended for poor and working-class readers, earning them the title "Kitchen Literature" because even servant girls could read them.

Bound books on the other hand were meant to last, be read multiple times, and carry knowledge across generations; books carried a cultural capital that newspapers did not.[7] In order to reinforce that distinction and create an American literature that was tied to books rather than serials, serious American authors trying to be published in books had to differentiate themselves from the serial authors. The first step toward this goal was to avoid low-brow language at all costs.

Linguistic choices communicate much more than ideas; they indicate who an idea is for and where it fits in the culture. Book publishers knew this and leveraged it to distinguish themselves from the cheap serials. The idea was that if books had more formal and error-free language, their place in the cultural hierarchy would be preserved and consumers would continue to purchase bound books as a symbol of cultural capital.[8] The strategy worked. Publishing houses stayed in

---

[7]Gross and Cohen, "Building a National Literature."

[8]Books as the containers for culture is an idea that has continued to persist. As recently as 2014, a massive international study was undertaken to assess whether there was a relationship between book ownership and educational attainment. It turns out that children of households with more books are

business publishing bound books while the cheap serials continued to meet public demand.[9] This also meant that books had to essentially ban slang and colloquial language. No problem—authors could still let their characters use informal language and regional dialects, it just couldn't be used to tell the story and they couldn't use any slang terms that might be mistaken as real words. OK was stuck in a gray area.

Unfortunately for us, there are exceedingly few original cheap serial publications remaining, so we have no way of knowing the prominence of OK in them. There are a few of the more famous ones housed in museums, but not nearly enough to determine the trends in vocabulary use of the time. Without any way of knowing, we must focus on the evidence we have from book revisions.

Let's return now to Henry David Thoreau and his attempt to write OK. An early draft of *Walden* from 1850 included this passage:

> When I ask for a garment of a particular form, my tailoress tells me gravely, "They do not make them so now," and I find it difficult to get made what I want, simply because

---

more successful in formal education, itself a codification of class and culture (Evans, Kelley, and Sikora).

[9] Gross and Cohen, "Building a National Literature"; King, "'Literature of the Kitchen.'"

she cannot believe that I mean what I say: it surpasses her credulity. Properly speaking, my style is as fashionable as theirs. "They do not make them so now," as if she quoted the Fates! I am for a moment absorbed in thought, thinking, wondering who *they* are, where *they* live. It is some Oak Hall, O call, O.K., all correct establishment which she knows but I do not.[10]

Clearly, he is being playful transforming Oak Hall, a clothing store, into O.K. and subsequently, all correct. OK must have been in Thoreau's vocabulary and culturally familiar enough to be worked into a joke. However, by the 1854 publication, he revised the passage, working the joke out of it:

When I ask for a garment of a particular form, my tailoress tells me gravely, "They do not make them so now," not emphasizing the "They" at all, as if she quoted and authority as impersonal as the Fates, and I find it difficult to get made what I want, simply because she cannot believe that I mean what I say, that I am so rash. When I hear this oracular sentence, I am for a moment absorbed in thought, emphasizing to myself each word separately that I may come at the meaning of it, that I may find out by what degree on consanguinity *They* are related to *me* . . .

---

[10]Metcalf, *OK*.

It is easy to view this passage and see how it was rewritten both for clarity and for tone. So maybe it was just a coincidence that OK was written out. However, that doesn't explain why OK didn't appear again in his writing and—to the best of our knowledge—it didn't appear in any other drafts until Louisa May Alcott tried to slip it into *Little Women* (where it was promptly edited out).

Thoreau and Alcott knew each other well. Their families were close, both lived in Concord, Massachusetts for a time, both were unconventional characters, and Thoreau was even Alcott's schoolteacher for a few years. Even as a child, Alcott was determined to be a writer. So, when her family moved to Boston, Alcott stayed behind to pursue her writing career. At first, she wrote under the pen name A. M. Barnard, producing fiction for the serial presses. She made enough to support herself and contribute to her family, but none of those early stories or poems garnered much attention. Nothing like *Little Women*, anyhow.[11]

As the story goes, Alcott didn't want to write *Little Women*; her publisher said that if she wrote a book for girls, he would publish her father's philosophy of education. So, to help get her father's work published, she wrote a semi-autobiographical work about coming of age in a household of girls.[12] Set during the Civil War, it is the story of four sisters, with one (Jo) loosely

[11]Reisen, *Louisa May Alcott*.
[12]Ibid.

based on Louisa May. It was an instant sensation, and she was asked to write a second volume almost immediately. Alcott's characters were realistic; they addressed contemporary issues and represented girls as they were: not as prudish and one-dimensional, but with depth and complexity.

This depth and complexity was reflected in their language. All the characters use colloquialisms and say things that were unladylike for the time, Jo most of all. She is so brash that the other characters comment on her use of slang and gentlemanly manners. OK was too much even for Jo. But Alcott didn't make Jo say OK—she put it in the mouth of the refined and artistic sister, Amy. In the 1869 version (of volume two), Amy writes a letter to her mother explaining that she will accept an offer of marriage:

> One of us must marry well. Meg didn't, Jo won't, Beth can't yet, so I shall, and make everything okay all round.[13]

By 1880, when the editors revised the book (making it more prim and proper), OK was edited out. Now, Amy would make things cozy rather than okay:

> One of us must marry well. Meg didn't, Jo won't, Beth can't yet, so I shall, and make everything cozy all round.

Alcott may have invented okay explicitly for this purpose; it is the first documented use of this spelling. But it is a

---

[13] Metcalf, *OK*.

hypercorrection. Hypercorrection is the non-standard use of language that results from over-applying a rule. It often occurs when trying to emulate more formal or higher-class forms of language. It can be grammatical ("Whom is coming to dinner?") but occasionally occurs in spelling. Surely Alcott knew "okay" was a hypercorrection for OK and may have written it that way for many different reasons. For example, she may have been ascribing the social practice of hypercorrection to Amy. Amy was studying art in Paris, but only because her aunt had the means to support her. She explicitly stated that she wanted to be more ladylike and was striving to be so: "You laugh at me when I say I want to be a lady, but I mean a true gentlewoman in mind and manners, and I try to do it as far as I know how."[14]

However, it could also be that Alcott was trying to appease her editors because they probably would not have allowed a slang word like OK into a printed and bound book. But okay was not OK and gave it the air of being more formal, a real word. Regardless, it was edited out in the second edition, swapped for the less controversial cozy.

In the end, it was likely a combination of business concerns and author tone that kept OK out of books. OK may have appeared in the cheap serials, which were held to different linguistic standards. But book readers would have to wait until the end of the century for okay to start appearing in mainstream books.

---

[14]Alcott. *Little Women.*

6 OH-KAY (TELEPHONE)

I AM a copper wire slung in the air,
Slim against the sun I make not even a clear line of shadow.
Night and day I keep singing—humming and thrumming:
It is love and war and money; it is the fighting and the tears,
the work and want,
Death and laughter of men and women passing through me,
carrier of your speech,
In the rain and the wet dripping, in the dawn and the shine
drying,
A copper wire.

–CARL SANDBURG, 1916

When Alexander Graham Bell patented the telephone in 1876, he probably knew it was going to change the world.[1]

---

[1] Bell has the first American patent for the telephone, but the actual inventor is debatable. Elisha Gray was working on the telephone at the same time.

But he probably did not know that it would have profound consequences for OK by giving it new life—as a discourse marker.[2]

Discourse markers are words that keep conversations going. They mark transitions, manage the flow of information, and express attitudes. Most spoken discourse markers (i.e., I mean, like, fine, good, great) have been repurposed from other parts of speech, and OK is no exception. OK is an adjective: it modifies nouns. Lots of discourse markers are adjectives (good, great), some are adverbs (now, anyway), and some are phrases (as I was saying). All except for OK have been in the language for a very long time; it is rare for young words to take on such important pragmatic functions. So how did OK get the role? The answer lies in the telephone.

The telephone transformed interpersonal communication. With a telephone, two people could be miles apart and still hear each other. This was so revolutionary that in the beginning, people often thought it was a trick. But it wasn't a trick: long-distance communication was moving out of the realm of durable, visible media (telegrams, letters, smoke signal, etc.) into an ephemeral, spoken one.

Gray and Bell's lawyers applied for the patent on the same day. Bell's lawyer was fifth on the list and Gray's was 39th. After many lawsuits, Bell got the patent, and Brown, Historical First Patents (Beauchamp, "Who Invented the Telephone?").

[2]Bell's research on the telephone was in service to the deaf community as both his mother and wife were deaf. Though he did invent hearing aids, the telephone, a tool leveraged by the hearing community, is his lasting legacy.

In the late 19th century, a group of technologies collectively transformed time and space: the railroad, the telegraph, and the telephone. The distant was becoming proximal in every way possible.

Railroads compressed time in a way that made it feel that all space was closing in on itself—the whole of the United States collapsed onto the East Coast and all of Europe onto Paris:

> Even the elementary concepts of time and space have begun to vacillate. Space is killed by the railways, and we are left with time alone. . . . Now you can travel to Orleans in four and a half hours, and it takes no longer to get to Rouen. [. . .] I feel as if the mountains and forests of all countries were advancing on Paris. Even now, I can smell the German linden trees; the North Sea's breakers are rolling against my door.[3]

By 1869, the U.S. intercontinental railroad was completed, drawing the American East and West coasts together.

This compression of space wasn't limited to travel—it happened in the news, too. The telegraph brought all the world's events to every small town, making global problems local, and drawing attention to the quickly expanding world and away from the immediate concerns of a local community. Not everyone embraced this transformation:

---

[3]Heinrich Hein, 1843, quoted in Schivelbusch, *The Railway Journey*, p. 34.

The little Alpena [Michigan] Echo cut off its daily telegraph service because it could not tell why the great head in the telegraph company caused it to be sent a full account of a flood in Shanghai, a massacre in Calcutta, a monkey dance in Singapore, a sailor fight in Bombay, hard frosts in Siberia, a missionary banquet in Madagascar, the price of kangaroo leather in Borneo, and a lot of nice cheerful news from the Archipelagoes, and not a line about the Muskegon fire.[4]

But technology steamed ahead, and by 1861, the transcontinental telegraph was completed, connecting the United States with Western Europe and theoretically the entire world.

No sooner did the telegraph make its way into nearly every town, the telephone was invented. The telephone compressed space and time in a more intimate way, by uncoupling the voice from the body, sending one without the other. It was such a radically new experience that it conjured feelings of existential dread (we might imagine a similar experience using video chat for the first time). People began asking what space was if the voice could be transmitted by electricity while the body was stationary:

---

[4] The *Detroit News*, 1891, quoted in Marvin, *When Old Technologies Were New*, p. 191.

We shall soon be nothing but transparent heaps of jelly to each other. . . . I look forward with doubtful pleasure to the time when I can sit by my own fireside and spy upon the doings of my friends and enemies in their homes two or three streets away.[5]

By 1877, telephones were being commercially produced and by 1910, there were 5.8 million connected telephones in the United States. It was an incredible transformation that changed the social fabric. The medium itself demanded new ways of communication, and together, the telegraph, railroad, and telephone created a perfect environment for the spread and evolution of OK.

The Telegraph

It seems like a distant memory in our collective psyche, but dispatching trains was a difficult problem. The train dispatcher in one city needed a way to communicate with the dispatcher in another to let them know the train was coming. This problem had a big impact on OK.[6]

---

[5] *Electrical Review*, 1891, quoted in *Pearson's Magazine*, p. 68.
[6] The solutions to this problem also forced standardization of timekeeping and time zones.

By 1851, most cities in the East Coast that had a train station also had a telegraph line (and accordingly, most telegraph lines were next to train tracks). Telegraphs were a perfect choice for dispatching trains: they were instantaneous even across large distances, and unambiguous because they were written. But every single letter in a telegraph had a cost, and conductors only needed to give their stamp of approval. They needed to indicate that everything was "ALL CORRECT," but at 10 letters, that phrase was a terrible choice. Fortunately, there was a well-known and popular (albeit somewhat derogatory) acronym for all correct: OK.[7] So, by 1855, OK was dispatching trains. In the 1855 annual report to stakeholders, the New York and Erie Railway Companies wrote:

> When two trains, running in contrary directions, are to be moved toward each other by special order, neither shall be permitted to start until Conductors and Engineers of both Trains shall have received "O. K." to a "32" message.[8]

No longer a joke or a political slogan, OK was at the center of the most sophisticated technology of the time. This imbued

---

[7]This is not the last time that a fringe cultural artifact became the standard in a new technology, just look to the Playboy centerfold of Forsén that, in 1973, became the standard jpeg test image. – *Kingster, Finding Lena*
[8]New York and Erie Company, *Annual Report*.

OK with a level of modernity no other word could achieve and gave it a prominent role in American infrastructure. OK had become a fixture of American vocabulary and culture. OK's importance and utility only increased once the telephone went mainstream.

The Telephone

When it was invented, the telephone was in direct competition with the telegraph. They both offered long-distance communication, but the telegraph did it better—or so many people thought. With the telegraph, clear, unambiguous communication could be achieved instantly across large distances at a relatively affordable price. By contrast, early telephone communication was very low quality and expensive. An unreliable and expensive technology was no match for a reliable and cheap one.[9] But using a telephone more closely approximates natural human communication and allows us to do a very important thing with language: connect.

In a conversation, many words are almost meaningless. They are questions asked out of politeness ("how are you?"), acknowledgment of actions ("please" and "thank you"), or

---

[9]Surely, this is why the president of Western Union rejected an early offer to buy the telephone's patent.

discourse markers to help signal that we are still listening ("hmm," "yep," "ok"). The primary purpose of this kind of language is to show that we care about the other person. The general term for this kind of language is phatic: language that is socially rich, but informationally empty.

Phatic language is not appropriate in a telegram; telegraphic communication is short and public. Telegraphs were billed per word, so there was only information and no pleasantries. Reading a telegram required a specially trained operator who knew Morse code, so there was no intimacy. This made telegrams perfect for dispatching trains and transmitting news, but terrible for maintaining social relationships.

Telephones, on the other hand, were billed per minute and allowed for more natural expression. Speech doesn't require an operator to decode, allowing for (somewhat) greater intimacy.[10] This made telephones perfect for social communication and terrible for dispatching trains and reporting the news.

But this new format also required new social norms. First, users had to say something when picking up the phone. They resorted to "hello?" (as advocated for by Thomas

---

[10]Early telephones were not private. Operators could listen or another party could be dropped into the line. But a telephone call did not depend on a third-party interpreter like a telegram did.

Edison) even though it was seen as horribly crass.[11] But people are willing to be crass and informal if it meets their communication needs.

This is where OK found its new identity. Maintaining a conversation without visual cues means vocalizing facial and body language. People needed to communicate messages like "continue" or "I understand you" or "that is all correct." They needed to be able to acknowledge the other person's statement, communicate that they still understood, and tacitly accept whatever was said—all without interrupting the flow of conversation. They needed a new discourse marker.

"Mm-hmm" is too difficult to hear on a weak connection and phrases interrupt conversation (especially with a slight delay), and "Ah" suffers from the same problem, but OK was a perfect candidate. To understand why requires understanding a little bit about human speech sounds.

How "loud" a sound is called its sonority. This is how much the vocal cords are involved in making the sound. Vowels are very sonorous. The consonants /p/, /t/, and /k/ are not sonorous at all. (Try putting your first 2 fingers on your throat while making these sounds—there shouldn't be

---

[11] By 1910, even AT&T was trying to suppress hello, publishing a hortatory essay on the matter: "Would you rush into an office or up to the door of a residence and blurt out 'Hello! Hello! Who am I talking to?' No, one should open conversations with phrases such as "Mr. Wood of Curtis and Sons wishes to talk to Mr. White . . . without any unnecessary and undignified 'Hello's'" (Marvin, 1990).

any vibration, then try making vowel sounds—there should be lots of vibration: that's sonority.)

OK is pronounced something like "oh-kay" and is about as extreme as a word can get, sound-wise. It's like a sonority sandwich. There are 2 very sonorous sounds surrounding the least sonorous sound possible. This contrast is what makes it so easy to hear—even on a poor connection. A word like "right," on the other hand is far less distinctive: The /r/ is somewhere in the middle of the sonority scale, the vowel, which sounds like /a/ and /i/ sandwiched together, is complicated, and though the final /t/ is not sonorous, nothing comes after it, so the listener has less to hear. On a poor connection, this is disastrous.

Furthermore, OK was efficient. "Yes, I agree with and approve of everything you just said" is an inefficient way to express OK. Even "all correct," with its three syllables, is longer than "oh-kay" with its two.

So, by 1902, OK was the standard across communication media. In an article about using telephones (as opposed to telegraphs) for collaboration and communication by railway companies, a verbal OK was an accepted stamp of approval—even for dispatching trains:

Why use a complex and artificial method of communication when a simpler and more direct [one] can be employed? What is simpler and more natural than to call an employee into your presence, dictate to him and order, which he writes out and reads over to you, and receives your "O. K." sanction? This, a good telephonic apparatus virtually does.[12]

And then if the line failed:

> Of course, if the line failed before "O. K." could be sent, those two momentous letters could not be written on the order by the operator or agent and it was marked, "void," and so forwarded to the dispatching office in the next morning's returns.

"Those two momentous letters," OK, momentous! The same author goes on to talk about the importance of "getting the O.K." and how easy it is to communicate instructions via the telephone. And a lot of instructions were needed. Railroads were spreading across the United States, and coordinating arrivals, departures, maintenance, etc. required a lot of communication. For the first part of the twentieth century, that communication was a mixture of telegrams and telephone calls with OK at the center. If everything was going as planned, the telegram would suffice: "32," "OK" and the train is off. If a dispatcher needed to change the plan or give specific instructions, the telephone was better because he could check for understanding. He could "get the O. K."

---

[12] Hammond, "The Railroad Telephone," p. 753.

But there was a bigger process going on across society: OK was becoming lexicalized.

Lexicalization

Lexicalization is when new words are created or added to a language. Typically, new words start out as temporary words used by a niche group of speakers: maybe they came from another language (like *bandanna* from Hindi/Urdu or *ombudsman* from Swedish) or they're a portmanteau (like *hangry*, from hungry and angry) or a brand name (like *google* or *dumpster*).

When exactly a word fully crosses the line from being a temporary word into being part of a language is a matter of debate within linguistics.[13] Whether OK was lexicalized by its role in the telegraph or by its role in the telephone is debatable, but by 1900, OK was an essential part of the American vocabulary.

Sitting at the intersection of telegraphs, telephones, and railroads, OK was also a symbol of modernity and sophistication. But evidence of its lexicalization wasn't limited to the new technologies: it made its way into the traditional ones, too. From 1880 until 1910, OK appeared

---

[13]Of course, exactly what is a language is also a matter of debate within linguistics.

more frequently in books, magazines, and pamphlets, fueled by the newfound purpose for this word.

Likewise, marketers everywhere wanted to brand their communication companies with OK. By 1905, there was O.K. Telephone Co. in Missouri and Minnesota (separate companies with the same name), O.K. Mutual Telephone Co. and O.K. Rural Telephone Co. both in Iowa, and O.K. Underground Distribution Box which provided underground telephone services for emergency personnel in Wisconsin. Not all the companies provided telephone services, OK had spread into the energy sector with The O.K. Electrical Construction Company in New York City. It also appeared in office supplies: The O.K. Manufacturing Co., Inc. in Syracuse New York made O.K. Paper Fasteners. In one pamphlet, The O.K. Manufacturing Co. used O.K. no fewer than 24 times to convince shop owners to sell their fasteners (which were apparently the most attractive fasteners available).[14]

But O.K. Telegraph Co. did not exist.

As OK became fashionable, it also became mainstream, appearing in even the most formal contexts such as indicating approval in congressional proceedings, land surveys, and the safety of pharmaceuticals. One medical pamphlet read "preparations marked O.K. contain no inhibited drug and require no supplemental label."[15] Likewise, official

---

[14] *Walden's Stationer and Printer.*
[15] Control, *The Budget Report of the State Board of Finance and Control to the General Assembly, Session of [1929-] 1937.*

government documents about everything from finances to fisheries used OK as a stamp of approval.[16] It had even become a verb by 1899, when one health report read, "he placed and embargo on the sale of milk unless the Chicago health department O.K.'d it at the farm."

A Modern OK

As soon as OK became mainstream and widespread, it became devoid of its earlier connotations of being a misspelling. In fact, its entire identity as an acronym was stripped from it. It had a denotation (the agreed-upon meaning that might be found in a dictionary i.e., yes, approved, all correct, etc.), but its connotation as a playful adaptation of "all correct" evoking spunky newspaper editors and smear politics was gone by the beginning of the 20th century.

But OK is resilient, and no sooner than it became boring, it got a face-lift and became fun again. This time, it got lengthened into oke, okey doke, okey dokey, and similar variations. These were fun, funny, playful, and slang. As quoted in a June 16, 1929 issue of the *Philadelphia Inquirer* article on slang (and quoted in Metcalf's work on OK):

As in non-collegiate circles, the ponderous O.K. has given way to the snappier "oke." There is a sonorous note about

---

[16]Health, *Annual Report of the State Board of Health of Indiana.*

this expression, the compiler says, which has made its vogue immense. Among elite slangsters, in fact, it has almost completely ousted older expressions.

If oke was slang, then OK couldn't be. And at the beginning of the 20th century, OK's periods were disappearing, suggesting that people considered it a word rather than an acronym. But this was not a period of extreme language play. The process that turned OK into oke, okey, oakey, oke doke, okey dokey, and more is a normal part of human behavior. People play with language; they invent slang, twist words, and adapt pronunciation and spelling all the time. Oke doke and its variations are all examples of human creativity, and they are examples of the creativity that is always there.

These OK variations are all a particular type of language play: diminutization. It is typical of toddler speech (produced by both toddlers and adults talking to toddlers), is closely associated with feminine speech, and happens in almost every language (though each language does it differently). In English, it is done by adding /i/, /ie/, or /y/ to the end of a word or doubling part or all of it ("pet the doggie" or "put on your shoe-shoe"). It can signal social intimacy, playfulness, or mockery.[17] But not every word is a candidate.

---

[17]Because diminutive forms exist in so many languages, researchers believe that they actually make language learning easier and may be a crucial part

Cross-linguistically, the most common diminutive words are nouns (birdie, doggie, shoe-shoes). Verbs are hard to make diminutive (eatie doesn't work very well, neither does workie unless it's a noun), and prepositions don't work at all (ofie makes no sense, and neither does atie). But discourse markers and interjections (like OK) take all sorts of interesting forms: nightie night, bye-bye, and okey doke.

This process has nothing to do with any technology: it is simply something that humans do with language. But we only do it with words that we are familiar with and readily understand. For OK, the diminutive and playful variations show us that OK was fully lexicalized.

But OK was still limited to the United States. It wasn't that English was confined to the United States: it was a global language even by 1900, as people living in the former and existing British Empire learned English. But OK had yet to make its way around the world. The next wave of technological and cultural changes would make it global and catapult it into being the world's most popular world, symbolic of an era of accelerated cultural exchange.

---

of human language acquisition (Jurafsky, "Universal Tendencies in the Semantics of the Diminutive.").

7 OK! (TELEVISION)

OK is global: A monolingual Japanese speaker and a monolingual Portuguese speaker don't have a lot of words in common. But most certainly they have three: "hello," "bye-bye," and OK. By the early 1990s, OK was understood by nearly every person on the planet (recall that Coca-Cola study from Chapter 4). In the short view, we see that television and the export of American culture via film and media played a major role in the spread of OK. But television was far from the first technology to play a role in the globalization of OK. To understand how OK spread, we need to understand what made English the global powerhouse it is today.

Like every other modern human language, English is the result of evolution, language contact, and political forces that reshaped the British Isles long before British colonization. The British Isles have been a multilingual, multicultural space for as long as people have recorded history. In 730 AD, there were five tribal groups, with five corresponding languages, each with a multitude of dialects. Old English (as the earliest state of modern English is now called) is the result of this diversity.[1]

By the fifteenth century, English, French, and Latin were the dominant languages. Educated people would have been fluent in all three. Most people would speak English at home, French for administrative tasks, and Latin in church. As more people continued to settle on the island, the linguistic diversity increased, and English began to emerge as the lingua franca. By the seventeenth century, English was well established as the dominant language, and as the British began to expand their empire, so too was English spread across the globe.[2]

In the seventeenth century, dialects were just dialects—they did not inherently signal social class. The eighteenth century changed all of that. British culture became focused on politeness, manners, and class, and these values were applied to language.[3] Simultaneously, the printing press was making books and reading material more accessible. As a result, grammar references, dictionaries, and pronunciation guides were written and obtained by those who could afford

---

[1]This is according to Bede's *Ecclesiastical History of the English People*, which is the most important early text for understanding Roman rule, Anglo-Saxon settlement and the evolution of the Church. Its publication is also widely considered the beginning of an English identity. Though this book was written in Latin, Bede also wrote extensively in English.
[2]Crystal, "English Worldwide."
[3]Crystal, "The History of English."

them. Following the rules in these guides signaled that one was educated and a member of the upper class; conversely, violating the rules signaled lower class status. Of course, these rules were created by speakers of certain dialects, thereby elevating those dialects at the expense of others.

The nineteenth century and the Industrial Revolution exacerbated these divisions, reinforcing upper over lower class manners as well as urban over rural sensibilities. But even British grammarians and wealthy urbanites couldn't stop language change, and when North America was settled, English started to evolve there, too. Then, in 1828 (50 years after the United States declared independence from the British Empire), Noah Webster published *Webster's Dictionary*, effectively declaring American English its own dialect with its own standards—standards that were just as valid as those from London.

It was a watershed moment for English. Until this point, British (upper class London) English was essentially the only published English. Correspondingly, it was the dominant form in education. Furthermore, since the British government occupied territories around the world, British English was essentially synonymous with Global English. When Webster's Dictionary was published, it didn't change any of those facts. But it did claim that there could be another way, that there could be many official Englishes.

But language—especially written language—is slow to change. Twenty years after the publication of *Webster's Dictionary*, American English started gaining traction in the United States, but only in the United States, and British remained the dominant variety globally throughout the nineteenth century. But, by the end of the twentieth century, American English had overtaken British.[4] So, what made American English—with its simplified spelling, colloquial tone, and garbled pronunciation—so popular?

Culture, Technology, and War

The twentieth century was marked by two world wars that forever shaped global politics and culture. The Second World War reshaped the geopolitical landscape by placing liberalism and democracy at the fore, and the United States fashioned itself both as a symbol of that liberalism and its global enforcer.[5] Even pre-WWII, the United States represented itself as a center of individuality, wealth, progress, tolerance, and optimism. These themes appear in books from the 1860s, Hollywood movies from the 1920s, and the American ideal of the self-made, successful businessman. Both during and after the War, these characteristics were promoted even more enthusiastically.

There were physical realities as well. When telephone lines were laid in Canada in the late nineteenth century, Canada

---

[4]Gonçalves et al., "Mapping the Americanization of English in Space and Time."

[5]Garson and Kegley, "The Rise and Rise of American Exceptionalism."

(a British colony) was treated as an extension of the United States. Toronto didn't connect directly to Vancouver, nor did it connect directly to Western Europe. Rather, both cities were treated as northward extensions of existing American lines.[6] So, when the United States entered World War II and emerged on the winning side, the stage was already set for American culture to take a leading role.

Furthermore, World War II devastated Europe; European government attention was focused on rebuilding efforts, not on cultural programs. So, while the United States carried on developing the technological advances that came out of the War, Europe and other wealthy countries were rebuilding. At the same time, the United States began welcoming immigrants with open arms, passing the War Brides act in 1946 and Displaced persons act in 1948, causing an influx of British English speakers to come to the United States, and a subsequent increase in the British variety locally. Meanwhile, there was an increase in the American variety abroad, possibly because of the influx of American English into families via letters and other correspondence.[7]

The cultural aftermath of the war affected the British Empire particularly hard. The years immediately following the war were marked by decolonization as people everywhere

---

[6]Moffett, *The Americanization of Canada.*
[7]Gonçalves et al., "Mapping the Americanization of English in Space and Time."

began to question the legitimacy of British rule. In 1947, India was the first country to gain their independence from British rule after the war. They were followed by 36 more Asian and African countries over the next 25 years.

This put the former British colonies in a difficult situation. They were simultaneously trying to rid themselves of the British colonial identity while entering the global economic and political landscape as sovereign nations. This entry required the use of a lingua franca. Since everyone in the newly independent countries had been educated in English for their entire lives, English was the obvious choice. However, language is a powerful marker of identity, and British English was closely associated with the British imperial powers. So, continued use of British English was a symbol of the former colonial rule.

People needed another option. Fortunately, American English was ready and waiting. Substituting American spelling and vocabulary could simultaneously symbolize a new, liberated, and modern identity while still communicating clearly. And so American English became the fashion both in post-colonial countries and by progressive-minded people all over the world. As English continued to evolve in the wide range of social and cultural contexts in which it was used, "Global English" spelling and vocabulary became increasingly American.[8]

---

[8]Gonçalves et al.; Pennycook, *English and the Discourses of Colonialism*.

Furthermore, because of its own history, American English had come to represent democracy, liberalism, and independent rule. The United States was, after all, also a former British colony that went on to become a global superpower.

Meanwhile, the United States and Russia were deeply engaged in the Cold War, and were battling for cultural, social, and political power in countries around the world. The primary export of this period was political ideology, culture, and language. Consuming media was one way to align with American culture and values.[9]

Throughout this period, the United States was exporting culture through government-sponsored programs and private industry. The government offered aid packages distributing food, medicine, books, and other supplies. They built infrastructure such as roads, hospitals, and schools. And they put people on the ground through programs such as Peace Corps. There were also technological feats to behold: Space missions, radio, television, the earliest computers, and missiles.

But the army at the front lines of the Cold War was made up of private companies. From the end of World War II until the fall of the Berlin Wall, American companies were invested in

---

[9]Americanization is not limited to media as consumer goods were also consumed and displayed as outward symbols of the same values. However, the consumption of consumer goods is less central to the spread of OK.

spreading democratic values and liberal identities as it meant their products would have a global consumer base.

The entertainment industry provided music, television shows, movies, and more.[10] Food and beverage offered soda, potato chips, and other packaged foods, and fashion offered the blue jean. Particularly in Russia and the Soviet Bloc, purchasing and wearing blue jeans and other products symbolized alignment with Western ideas of government and culture.

In the 1980s, it was not uncommon to walk into a shop in Southeast Asia or a hair salon in East Africa playing Alabama or Madonna, or to walk through town and see a subtitled version of *I Love Lucy* playing on a television. By 1987, 79 percent of all television and film exports originated in the United States.[11]

For many people outside of the United States, television represented a gateway to another world, and English media was a form of education. Subtitles were instrumental in making television and film accessible. In the pre-internet era (and still today), countless people used those subtitles to learn English. And with so much media being produced in American English, learners had access to nearly endless engaging, well-produced English learning material (even if they was pedagogically lacking). However, in every language, there are a few words that don't translate well. OK is one of those.

---

[10]Puttnam, *Movies and Money*.

[11]Wagnleitner, *Coca-Colonization and the Cold War*.

But fortunately for OK, it is easy to hear and pick out of a conversation and it's easy to understand the meaning. In a stream of English speech, OK stands out, and it happens a lot—both at the beginnings and ends of phrases. OK also very often gets a unique intonation since it can be used to confirm a statement, check for understanding, introduce a topic change, and is otherwise set apart from the rest of an utterance. This salience has worked in OK's favor. A word that is short, easy to hear, easy to say, and appears multiple times in a conversation is easier to learn than a verb or noun that doesn't have all of these characteristics.

Of course, every language has a word that means something like OK. There's *d'accord* in French, but that is more like agreed. There's *vale* in Spanish, but that is more like all right. There's 我同意 (wǒ) in Chinese, but that's more like I agree, and there's *sawa* in Swahili which is also like all right. The list goes on, but OK has a special kind of utility, both because it can occur in so many contexts and because it has a discourse function that makes it difficult to translate.

So, television shows kept OK—even in the subtitles. And OK continued to spread. Thus, OK had gone global, and because of global politics, American culture had become internationally fashionable.[12] This worked in OK's favor

---

[12]Wagnleitner, *Coca-Colonization and the Cold War*; Puttnam, *Movies and Money*; Gonçalves et al., "Mapping the Americanization of English in Space and Time."

because while consumer goods may have been an easy and relatively cheap way to signal alignment with liberal ideas, language is free.

Humans do a lot with language. We use it to communicate thoughts and ideas, of course, but we also use it to portray identity. Word choice above all is a powerful way to communicate affiliation with social groups, identities, and ideologies. For example, a Soviet, German, or Italian teenager in the 1960s might have indicated their worldliness or liberal stance by using OK. Today this might look like a pronunciation choice when saying the name of a country.

Likewise, language has the added benefit of being easy to conceal. If someone was to signal their political or social affiliation, using OK was a great way to do it. Unlike Levi's jeans and Coca-Cola, which have a physical presence, it's possible to use language in one context (like with friends) and not in another (like with conservative parents, teachers, or officials) without there ever being a trace. And so, OK spread with television and liberal democracy: a symbol of Americanization.

8 K (THE INTERNET)

While most of the world was learning about OK through television, film, and music, researchers in the United States and United Kingdom were laying the foundation for the next big technology that would reshape OK yet again: the internet.

The need for a massive, distributed communication network originally began with fears about a nuclear confrontation between the United States and the United Soviet Socialist Republic (USSR). If a nuclear attack destroyed the central nodes in a communication network, the rest of the network would be rendered useless. The best way to prevent this was to develop a distributed, decentralized network. Telephones and telegraphs were completely dependent upon a few critical nodes and therefore were very vulnerable, the internet is not.

The basic ideas underpinning a distributed communication technology were developed simultaneously in at least three different organizations during the 1960s: The RAND Corporation and MIT in the United States, and the National Physical Laboratory (NPL) in the United Kingdom. But ultimately, it was the Defense Advanced Research Projects Agency (DARPA) who took the lead. DARPA had all the right tools to bring the internet to life. It had researchers from MIT, funding from the United States government, and the political motivation to create something sustainable.

So, DARPA created ARPANET and began connecting computers. By the end of 1969, the technology and infrastructure underpinning the internet was established.

Throughout the 1970s, more and more nodes (in the form of research centers) were added to the network. Just like when the railroads expanded, this new technology required new levels of coordination. But this time, the communication system needed to be integrated with the technology itself to facilitate the new type of communication. So, in 1972, internet researchers proposed electronic mail (AKA email). Initially, it was a simple send and read system, but it grew quickly, and by the end of 1973, users could send, read, file, forward, and respond to messages. By early 1974, users could attach files, and email was mostly complete.

It was an enormous success! Even the most popular apps today don't compare. Within 2 years, 75% of all traffic on ARPANET was email, and within 5 years, developers realized that email was ARPANET's real purpose.

Still, ARPANET and therefore email was only used by researchers and scientists, and—like the communication of railway engineers—it involved a lot of instructions, file transfers, and other practical exchanges. It's the type of communication that requires an acknowledgment of receipt, communication of understanding, and basic acceptance: the kind of communication that OK did for the railroads.

Unfortunately, those early messages are lost to history, and we cannot inspect them for traces of OK. We could ask the authors, but their recollection is (understandably) incomplete and hazy. In 1993, when interviewed by the Associated Press, Ray Tomlinson (who contributed the most to the invention of email) recalled that:

The first message was sent between two machines that were literally side by side. The only physical connection they had (aside from the floor they sat on) was through the ARPANET. I sent a number of test messages to myself from one machine to the other. The test messages were entirely forgettable and I have, therefore, forgotten them. Most likely the first message was QWERTYUIOP or something similar. When I was satisfied that the program seemed to work, I sent a message to the rest of my group explaining how to send messages over the network. The first use of network email announced its own existence.

We can forgive Tomlinson his fuzzy memory; surely he couldn't have known that his experiment would set off a radical cultural shift that would permanently alter human communication.[1] By the end of the 1970's, everyone involved

---

[1] Tomlinson also chose the @ sign. Of that choice he said, "The @ sign seemed to make sense. I used the @ sign to indicate that the user was 'at' some other host rather than being local."

knew that email would be the most transformative technology to emerge from ARPANET and a new communication medium was born.

As we've already seen, when new media arise, people need the vocabulary to manage interaction as well as communicate information. OK had been used as a discourse marker (those little words that keep a conversation going—see Chapter 6) since the advent of the telephone. Discourse markers are particularly vulnerable to the whims of communication. Nouns, verbs, adjectives, and prepositions evolve relatively slowly, but discourse markers adapt quickly to changing communication media.[2] As a discourse marker, OK's usage was once again reshaped by email, and the way we think about OK today still bears these traces.

Email altered three major dimensions of communication: speed, permanence, and formality. Speed is obvious. Before email, sending a file, manuscript, or any written instructions or other material took somewhere between days and months. With email, it took seconds to hours (early email was much slower than its modern form).

Second, email created a permanent record of correspondence like traditional written mail. Once a message was in the 'mailbox' it couldn't be altered.[3] This created

---

[2] Since language is a comparatively new phenomenon in human history, slowly is a relative term.
[3] Also Tomlinson's term.

a level of permanence in a digital space that mirrored the physical world. An email could be treated the same way as a document—with the same legal standing as physical mail, but easily searchable (once that capability was invented).

It was the best aspects of both the telephone and the telegram: quick and permanent. There was only one question remaining: What should emails look like? Should they be formal like a letter, informal like a telephone call, some hybrid, or completely different? Here, central ARPANET figures C.R. Linklider and Albert Vezza had an opinion:

> One of the advantages of the message systems over letter mail was that, in an ARPANET message, one could write tersely and type imperfectly, even to an older person in a superior position and even to a person one did not know very well, and the recipient took no offense. . . . Among the advantages of the network message services over the telephone were the fact that one could proceed immediately to the point without having to engage in small talk first, that the message services produced a preservable record, and that the sender and receiver did not have to be available at the same time.[4]

Clearly, they favored an informal but direct tone. They proposed that even strangers could jump right in and not

---

[4] Leiner et al., "A Brief History of the Internet."

waste time with things like lengthy introductions, small talk, or other "non-essential" communication. They were focused on language for exchanging information, not language for social connection. In their imagining, even typos would be completely acceptable in this new format.

To a certain extent, they were correct. A typo in an email is often perceived as less egregious than a typo in a more formal correspondence like a contract or bill. But the social standards of email evolved quickly, and once it was available to the public, etiquette guides emerged to corral users.

But for OK, it's the email developers' focus on direct communication that is so interesting. Railroad engineers expressed the same sentiment about the telephone. Their goal was not social connection, but communication of instructions, processes, and other practical information. For early email users, a message that simply acknowledged receipt with "Ok." was probably acceptable—and even desirable. Yet 40 years later, the purpose of email has changed, and that same message might be interpreted as terse or rude.

It's hard to see what people do in email because email is typically private. However, there is a public collection of over 600,000 emails: the Enron Corpus. Enron was an energy company about the size of Chevron, Goldman Sacks, or Microsoft before it disintegrated in a financial scandal. The Enron Corpus emails were created as part of the natural course of business from early 2000 to December 2001; they were collected as part of an investigation into Enron's accounting practices.

Investigators looked through all communication, including all correspondence between anyone in a leadership role. Enron had been an innovative early adopter of digital technologies and especially conducting work via email, so those documents included a lot of email.

Most of the emails were short and social, the digital banter of a modern office. There is evidence of friendships, romance, gossip, and plans for lunch. Reading through them is an eerie experience because it quickly becomes clear that no one thought these messages would ever be read. Though people were given an opportunity to withdraw their emails before the corpus was made public, most people left them in. As a result, the corpus is a snapshot into the lives of Enron leadership from 2000 to 2001. For example:

Subject: Re: Re[12]:

Date: 2000-09-08T04:34:00

From: Matthew <matthew.lenhart@enron.com>

To: jilallen@dttus.com

how was last night? sorry i didn't make it. i was planning on going but i got home late. i did check out woody's. it was ok. when do you leave for okla?

The economy of language that the email developers anticipated is gone. Most of the conversation is social and phatic (see Chapter 6). It is informal and riddled with typos as expected, but the purpose is to connect, not to exchange information. How emails became so social involves another technology, BBS's, which we will return to shortly.

In this corpus, "please" is the most common word, followed by "would," "enron," and "thanks." OK (and its variants, excluding abbreviations for Oklahoma) is 225th. Considering there are over 250,000 unique words, OK is in the top 0.1%. But, like "please," and unlike "thanks," it almost never occurs as a standalone message. (When it does, it is in a strictly social conversation, and someone is angry.) For example:

Subject: RE: Friday's report

Date: 2001-08-21T14:05:10

From: Ward, Kim S (Houston) <houston .ward@enron .com>

To: karla_dailey@city.palo-alto.ca.us

ok - not a problem. Kim

OK is so prominent in this corpus because it is so prominent in language generally. In the first example (from Matthew), it's an adjective. In the second (from Kim), it's an adverb, and in this one (from Shelley) it is a discourse marker.

Subject: Re: Calendar

Date: 2002-01-18T10:28:52

From: Corman, Shelley <shelley.corman@enron.com>

To: ricki.winters@enron.com

Ok I'm thru with appointment and am on my way in ---
---------------------- Sent from my BlackBerry Wireless
Handheld (www.BlackBerry.net)

In this way, the corpus reflects the language of 2001—language that has continued to shape email ever since. Beginning in 2018, most email providers (most importantly, Gmail) began offering Smart Compose and Smart Reply. Both features are presented to users as "helpful suggestions" for composing and replying to emails. The suggestions are the output of machine learning algorithms which were originally trained on the Enron Corpus.[5] Since then, every input to the system is just an adjustment to what the algorithm originally learned from the original corpus. As a result, the suggestions offered by Smart Compose and Smart Reply today are influenced by the social and cultural norms of 2001.

The Enron Corpus has been studied extensively to understand organizational communication, speech acts, and gender dynamics in the workplace. It has defined email both as legally binding documents and as a cultural practice. But the Enron Corpus is neither the beginning nor the end of email's tale and its relationship to OK. The social and cultural norms for email, short messaging, and discussion boards were not constrained to the vision of their inventors,

---

[5]Herrman, "You already email like a robot—Why not automate it?".

but were crowd sourced from the early adopters of BBSs of the 1980s and 90s.

Bulletin Board Systems

Bulletin Board Systems—BBSs for short—bridged the gap between telephone and internet service for the public. BBSs were local servers that users could dial into to connect with other users. They were very popular in the 80s and early 90s and were maintained by individual hobbyists rather than institutions.

BBS users exchanged messages privately and publicly, synchronously and asynchronously. They could post to message boards, visit chat rooms, chat one-on-one, and send private messages directly. The social norms of the internet were established in these early BBSs, as users adapted to this new rapid ability to communicate socially via writing. The only caveat was that most connections were with people nearby. A call to a BBS was charged the same way that a telephone call was, so users tended to cluster geographically (since long-distance telephone calls were more expensive).

In retrospect, this localization had some interesting consequences. First, colloquial and regional language was widely used and easily understood. Second, a sense of community created an air of informality. This level of informality was documented by the BBSs themselves. A moderator of one of the most popular BBSs, FidoNet, even posted standards for what things like "BCNU," "L8R," and ":P" meant ("been seeing you," "later," and "sticking out tongue," respectively). Though FidoNet was the most widespread and international of the BBSs, its norms were still heavily influenced by the smaller, more localized BBSs.

More so than the first internet researchers, these early BBS hobbyists established the rules and norms for communication that the modern internet evolved from. Paging through the records, it is not uncommon to find the typos that Linklider and Vezza predicted. However, there is also lots of the social communication, greetings, and pleasantries that they hoped email would obfuscate the need for. Vezza and Linklider hadn't accounted for the fact that when a new communication technology is adopted by large groups of diverse people, they do what they have always done: socialize.

This socialization led to a dramatic rise in language play, on par with—or even surpassing—the linguistic playfulness of the 1840s Penny Press revolution. The public bulletin boards were full of acronyms, abbreviations, emoticons, and other creative adaptations of written language (assumedly the private ones were too, though there are few surviving transcripts available to validate that claim). In this playfulness, nothing was sacred: people would abbreviate and respell almost anything. But greetings, closings, and discourse markers were all particularly susceptible to transformation. And of course, OK was, too.

Phatic phrases (such as greetings and discourse markers) are particularly susceptible to adaptation because they are formulaic, predictable, and social. This means that modifying them, adjusting them, and reinterpreting them doesn't interfere with communication of thoughts and ideas, though it does allow authors to signal social closeness and community.[6] Armed with creativity and an inspiring new communication platform, people went to work playing with language, establishing common acronyms, trying out doomed ones, and generally making their mark on the social norms of this new world.

OK was along for the ride. It was already extremely widespread, one of the most common words in the English language, used globally, and easily understood by most people on the planet. To this point, OK had already been adapted in informal situations to be spoken as 'kay' or 'mmm-kay' and their variations. However, in a pre-BBS world, there were few opportunities for informal written communication.[7] The BBS users were at the forefront of figuring out the social norms.[8]

---

[6]McSweeney, *The Pragmatics of Text Messaging*.

[7]There was, of course, lots of informal writing before BBSs: postcards, notes, physical bulletin boards, etc. However, the *amount* of written language being produced was completely unprecedented. By the beginning of 2020, the average young adult sent over 500 words a day in text/chat messages alone, say nothing of writing on other media (McSweeney).

[8]In the 1980s and 90s, BBSs were widely available in the United States and Canada, Western Europe, and Japan. The social norms that they were establishing—and even the encoding system to render letters and characters—come from this cultural lens. While not a homogeneous group, it is exclusive and mostly English-speaking (as a first, second, or other

They chose "K" (typically written in lowercase) as their abbreviation for the abbreviation, OK. They could have chosen "kay" or "keh"or even "mk." However, all of these are longer than the shortest form of the original, making them poor candidates as abbreviations. Following the convention of using the first letter of a word to represent it in an abbreviated form, they could have chosen "o." However, in English, there was already a discourse marker that began with, and sounded like, "o": "oh."

Other acronyms were multipurpose (i.e., *l.o.l.* for laugh out loud and lots of love), but LOL is typically recoverable from its context, whereas o would not necessarily be. Finally, they weren't abbreviating OK, they were abbreviating the spoken word, "kay," and the best abbreviation for kay is its first letter, K.

Even better, the English alphabetic pronunciation of the letter, K is just that. But K doesn't have the universality and versatility that OK does. For example, "k" in Spanish is an excellent abbreviation for the short preposition, *que*, which when spoken, also sounds like the English alphabetic pronunciation of k (a fact bilingual speakers play with extensively).[9]

---

language). Surely had it not been largely in English, OK wouldn't have been as popular.

[9]McSweeney, "Bilingual Youth Texts Corpus."

Today, a message of just k in an email would be read as excessively terse except in rare social situations. Even if we look to other digital platforms, a simple k is no longer acceptable, but "kk" is. But where did "kk" come from? For that, we have to look at how social media and synchronous chat combined to give OK new life.

9 KK (SOCIAL MEDIA)

To give some context to how OK ended up as KK, okie, okieeeeee, and other variations, we actually need to look back at the 1920s. The 20s marks the moment when OK lost any trace of its historical context among mainstream users. By this point, it was fully lexicalized, and therefore was a completely average word. It didn't have any connotations of misspellings, politicians, or even rowdy gangs. So, to imbue it with playfulness, the acronym itself had to be played with.[1] This is when oke doke, okey doke, okey dokey, and its variations emerged.[2]

In the early twenty-first century, people played with language—a lot! Anywhere there was the internet, language was changing. It was a high point of linguistic creativity, fueled by the advent of social media and widespread adoption of the internet and synchronous communication.[3]

---

[1]Metcalf, *OK*.

[2]The most extreme of these variations is possibly "okalie dokalie," a variation that was popularized Ned Flanders in *The Simpsons*, an animated television Show from the 1990s.

[3]McSweeney, *The Pragmatics of Text Messaging*.

Social media often gets the credit (or blame) for transforming society and correspondingly, language. As we shall see, however, the story is a little more complicated, and it has as much to do with the way the internet and smart phones evolved as it has to do with social media. It just so happened that these technologies arose in quick succession.

In 1997, the first social media site, sixdegrees.com, launched. Six Degrees allowed users to create profiles, send and receive messages, list acquaintances (i.e. friends, family, and other contacts), and see the links in the network (the chain) that connected them to any other user on the site. At its peak, Six Degrees had about 3.5 million registered users (enormous for 1997, but tiny by modern-day standards, and not enough to affect linguistic conventions). Six Degrees had all the right elements to be a successful social media site, but the infrastructure of the internet and personal computing was not ready to handle social media, and the site ultimately failed.

After Six Degrees, Myspace emerged. Myspace marked the beginning of what would become recognizable as social media by today's standards.[45] Like Six Degrees, Myspace allowed users to create a personal page showcasing their

---

[4]Friendster actually launched a year before Myspace, but Myspace was bigger. LinkedIn launched the same year as Myspace, but LinkedIn was both smaller and dedicated to professional networking rather than personal relationships, and therefore does not figure into the story of OK at this time.
[5]Also called "the social web," "Web 2.0," and more. We will stick with "social media."

interests and social connections. It was music and media-forward, allowing users to play a song whenever someone visited their page, and filling the screen with flash animation and creative features. With over 115 million users at its peak in 2008, Myspace transformed how people used the internet.

The first way it transformed the internet was its business model. Myspace was run by a private company and was free to use. Like an old school Penny Press, it made money by selling advertisements; unlike a Penny Press, it got its content for free from users. Second, it established many of the social norms around social media. For example, it became completely acceptable to visit someone else's page without alerting them to your presence. In fact, one could transverse an entire network of people, getting to know intimate details of their lives without ever letting them know. Likewise, it made sharing the most intimate details of one's life publicly completely normal.

With this model, millions of people collectively created billions of words. Myspace itself had linguistic conventions depending on age, gender, interests, and other characteristics. Unlike BBSs, which were regional and therefore replicated regional language, Myspace was international. So, while networks were still geographically localized (because friendships were still influenced by geography), they didn't have to be, and networks of distributed users began popping up around common interests.[6]

---

[6]This is a bit of a simplification: gaming communities have existed longer than social media, bringing people together around a common goal of

Just like all other communities, members needed a way to signal that they were a community. And just like all other communities, they used language to do so.[7] Language is an effective way to mark group membership; by using non-traditional spelling, abbreviations, or other orthographic conventions, individuals signal affiliation with a particular community or identity.

So, as geographically separated communities began to form around shared interests rather than shared physical space, language began to take center stage as a way to signal group membership and project an identity. The best words to do this fall into two categories: specialist terms, and words that are easily recoverable from context. Knowledge of specialist terms just means that someone has done their research and knows the associated vocabulary with a subgroup or special interest. Whether the topic is music, cars, or card games, knowing and being able to use the proper vocabulary is essential to gaining entry. These words are not typically candidates for transformation. They may be abbreviated, and they may be written as acronyms (as anyone who has ever started a new job will know, every community has their acronyms), but knowledge—not transformation—of them signals group membership.

---

playing a game. However, a much smaller portion of western society was involved in Massive Multiplayer Games than was involved in social media.
[7]McSweeney, *The Pragmatics of Text Messaging.*

Secondly, there are the words that can be easily recovered from context. This is where OK comes in. There were two standard forms in circulation: OK (with and without periods, upper and lower case) and okay. Both forms could be used as discourse markers, interjections, and adjectives (though some individuals try to make an artificial distinction between them). However, the discourse marker and interjection forms of OK take on the extra responsibility of modification. Modifying the adjective form is less common.

Let's look at some examples using okey doke. In a survey of 200 native English speakers from across the world, 100% of people found (1) and (2) to be acceptable, but only about 40% thought (3) was acceptable.

(1) Want to go to the movies?

   Okey doke! [interjection]

(2) [silence]

   Okey doke, let's get started! [discourse marker]

(3) How was the movie?

   It was okey doke! [adjective]

Even though participants didn't reject the adjective form in example 3 completely, they were uncomfortable with a non-traditional form in the adjective position. This is typical for language play: discourse markers and interjections are excellent candidates for modification since they typically manage a conversation more than communicate new information. However, adjectives typically communicate new information, so altering them may compromise the complete message.[8]

But back to 2003: Myspace was booming, people were putting themselves on the internet, and there was more written content being produced than ever before. At that time, it was the sheer volume of words people were writing that was driving language change. But Myspace was lots of simultaneous monologues, it was not designed for conversation. So, while communities formed through their Myspace networks, OK evolved in conversation, where people had the chance to communicate directly with others.

When Myspace started in 2003, the most popular platform for online conversation was AOL Instant Messenger (AIM). AIM allowed quick interactions with people users already knew or had contact information for. At its peak in 2001, there were 36 million users, but was not a networking site and it couldn't even be called social media since users didn't create anything except conversation. There were no profiles, no images; just avatars, buddy lists (that displayed who was online at the same time), and away messages. It was a communication platform and as such, it was transformational for OK and digital communication.

The contribution AIM made to social media was about displaying the synchronicity. This technology was one of

---

[8]Ibid.

their most valuable patents, and what differentiated AIM from a chatroom. By displaying who else in your network was online, AIM prioritized real-time conversation. It meant that users didn't have to coordinate to communicate: they could just check in to see who was available. There was a lot of hanging around, waiting for someone to chat with. AIM had become a digital hangout.

Prior to AIM, acronyms for greetings and leave takings were in active use: "brb" for "be right back," "ttyl" for "talk to you later," and other similar acronyms were formally documented in the Bulletin Board Systems as early as the 1980's.[9] However, AIM created the social context for them to be useful: with near-synchronous conversation playing a major role in social life, quick typing and fluency with abbreviations and acronyms were essential skills. It was the perfect environment for language change for many reasons. Teenagers and young adults are typically at the forefront of language evolution, and they were the most avid users of AIM.[10] Second, it was a new communication technology, which sparks new ways of communicating.[11] Finally, it was

---

[9]Edel, "MO_ICONS_PLEASE"; Bush, "FidoNet: Technology, Use, Tools, and History."

[10]Labov, "Social and Language Boundaries among Adolescents"; Merchant, "Teenagers in Cyberspace."

[11]Baron, "Instant Messaging and the Future of Language."

conversational, which means new forms spread quickly through networks.[12]

In response, nearly every variation of OK imaginable can be found in these chat logs. The list is practically infinite because each variation listed here can be written with any number of capital or lowercase letters, any amount of repetition of any letter or string of letters (though the last letter is the most common to repeat), any combination of sub-parts (i.e., "okey" in okey doke can become "okeh" to make okeh doke) and any amount of intervening punctuation (not limited to periods, but also including exclamation points, hyphens, etc.).

The root forms are:

- OK (traditional)
- Okay (classic)
- K (efficient)
- KK (fun)
- AC (nerdy)
- Kay (transcribed speech)
- Oh Kay (longer transcription)
- Oke (historic)

---

[12]Paolillo, "'Conversational' Codeswitching on Usenet and Internet Relay Chat."

- Okey (playful)
- Oh Key (playful and transcribed and a pun!)
- A-OK (playful and nerdy)
- Okie / okie dokie (cute)
- Okeh (historic and playful)
- Oki / oki doki (cute and efficient)
- OKs (literal)
- Oke doke
- Okey dokey
- Okalie dokalie (inefficient!)
- and more.

The sheer breadth of creativity is staggering, and it wasn't just happening on AIM: anywhere people congregated to communicate, language play was present. This creativity would have been confined to interactions between individuals and small groups it weren't for social media. Social media provided the context for the rapid explosion in text and visual communication that defined the early twenty-first century. The combination of synchronous chat like AIM and social media helped spur this transformation.

With the widespread adoption of platforms like Myspace, people (in the wealthiest countries) were connected around common interests rather than geography. Users were tasked with forging communities that centered around interests, professions, hobbies, and identities. There were groups for Jazz music lovers and World War I dabblers, musicians and accountants, quilters and Anime collectors, gay men and young adults who feel a connection to the 1960s. It was the first time in recorded history that people could easily connect without geography. Social media was transformational because it allowed groups to form around relatively uncommon thoughts, feelings, and experiences. But the members of these communities were tasked with a challenging job: to establish a group identity without shared space.

Fortunately, they had language. Linguistic creativity helps people establish in-group and out-group membership, and it took center stage at this point in the internet's (and OK's) evolution. The same as with BBSs: knowledge of a community's slang and acronyms (or technical terms) was essential to signaling membership to other members of a group. Using those terms—even in a private conversation—reinforces those ties. Because they are often opaque to out-group members, it also serves to exclude people who do not have that knowledge.

This aspect of human language has existed likely since languages have and is an effective way to quickly get a sense of what group someone belongs to. This was particularly important during the earliest stages of social media because it also served a warranting function. Warranting is validating that someone is who they say they are and is often accomplished by referencing specific aspects of one's offline life in online contexts. Social media sites have since incorporated more opportunities for warranting (i.e. by displaying locations and other personal details, listing interests across categories, cross-linking social media profiles, etc.), but a properly placed "okieeee" serves a similar function, validating the fact that someone is involved in the communities that they say they are.

And again, the way OK is used today still bears the effects of this social dynamic. After being established in conversational spaces, these varieties spread, and because slight nuances in how someone spells OK can help signal group membership, they spread like wildfire anywhere warranting was needed

But that wasn't the only force spreading variations of OK around the world. Due to the fact that English played (and still plays) such a central role in the internet, English words and phrases have an out-sized digital presence.

English (particularly American English) became the default lingua franca of the internet for a lot of reasons. First, the technology was developed among English speakers, and because DARPA played such a central role in establishing the standards (DARPA was an American government program) English was the language of development. So, the small decisions that have a big impact (like character encoding) were designed to handle English first. It is completely possible that the early inventors of the internet never thought that their creation would be so central to the global economy or that speakers of nearly every human language would be online. But by not having that foresight or knowledge, they made decisions that would forever shape how languages are encoded digitally.

Second, having a computer with an internet connection required a lot of infrastructure, wealth, and social capital. Because the United States is both wealthy and large, a lot of the early users were based in the United States, and a lot of the content they generated was written in American English. This primordial privilege of English established norms of communication that continue to influence digital communication today. From widely used acronyms that are still borrowed into other languages (i.e. "okieeee" and "lol") to the official Unicode title of emojis (i.e. "Ok Hand Sign Emoji")[13], they were based on English.

Finally, the programming languages that are used to build the internet (Lisp, PHP, HTML, CSS, JavaScript) are based on English. Again, it's a small decision, but privileges English speakers because it is easier to learn what a <div> tag does if you already know what a division is.

The English-oriented nature of the internet and correspondingly social media only reinforced the post-colonial ubiquity that English already enjoyed. But this time the consequences of English first would continue to shape the

---

[13] Though most screen readers can translate most emojis' Unicode titles, they were titled for an English-speaking audience.

global culture via the internet. It also gave English a priority status, and the number of Global English speakers has continued to grow. Even as the United States population growth has started to slow (and decline), the American variety of English has been taken up as a second language around the world.

The universality of English on the internet was advantageous for OK's creative adaptations as well. The playful, creative forms listed above frequently appear in non-American media such as Japanese manga. It is difficult to say if these forms originated in manga or were just adopted by the community, but these playful forms of OK help signal group membership to anyone who recognizes them. In this way, they are hiding in plain sight.

The various forms of OK help like-minded people find each other in unexpected places. It may be an interaction between friends or co-workers, but when someone uses a non-traditional form of OK, they are subtly signaling the social groups they are affiliated with. Though the connotations won't be understood by everyone, other in-group members will recognize the association, whether they are consciously aware of it or not. As we shall see, this effect extends to the gesture as well.

As the internet is further ingrained into daily life for many, these linguistic cues become increasingly important in developing relationships and establishing trust and community. In this way, creative adaptations are functional tools to preserve our social relationships, and in turn, our humanity in a digitally mediated world.

10 👌 (GESTURE)

So far, we have focused on OK the word, the stories it tells, the baggage it carries, and the changes it has seen. Many words carry these tales, but OK is so big that it transcends language into gesture, crossing over from a widely used word into an internationally recognized hand symbol. It is so widespread that it has its own origin myth and even became an emoji.[1] OK as a hand gesture has a different story than OK as a word. The hand gesture connects our modern world—with all its complexity, social tensions, and ambiguity—with a shape that is deeply rooted into the human experience. The OK gesture is bigger than OK, but its relationship to OK today illustrates just how complicated language—and gesture—can be.

The OK gesture is part of the oldest documented class of hand gestures: ring gestures. Ring gestures are the class of hand shapes made by the index finger touching the thumb to create a ring or circle (sometimes the index finger and

---

[1] At the time of writing, there are approximately 1800 emoji listed by Unicode, and approximately 30 of those are hand gestures.

middle finger both touch the thumb). What happens with the remaining fingers is what makes each ring gesture distinct. For OK, the remaining three fingers are straight and separated, and the gesture is typically displayed with the palm facing out.

Ring gestures have been documented and defined globally since the fifth century BC both in Buddhist texts and in European imagery.[2] They have served a variety of purposes, from the divine to the secular, the beautiful and the vulgar; sometimes just one can serve all of them.

In most English-speaking countries and in most contexts, the OK gesture is similar the word, assenting, agreeing, and confirming. However, in other cultures and contexts, it can carry extremely positive (or negative) connotations.

The negative connotations include the vulgar or lewd as in Venezuela, Brazil, Sardinia, Modern Greece, and Malta where it refers to sex and sexuality in various derogatory ways.[3,4] In France, the gesture is a personal insult, used to say that someone is "a zero" or worthless. In the United States, where it can be read as a political symbol of hatred.

Around 2015 in the United States, the OK gesture was adopted by some prominent alt-right figures as a symbol of

---

[2]Saunders, "Symbolic Gestures in Buddhism"; Müller, "Ring-Gestures across Cultures and Times."

[3]Müller.

[4]Morris, *Peoplewatching*.

unity among white supremacists.[5] They saw the letters, /w/ and /p/ in the gesture, and used it to stand for white people. The w is in the upright figures, and the p is in the closed forefinger and thumb with the tail of the p extending into the wrist (it takes some imagination). But its alt-right connotation wasn't widely known until 4chan users (4chaners) pushed it into the spotlight.[6] In 2017—in an act that can only be described as trolling—4chaners flooded the internet with the OK gesture saying that OK stood for white people. They described the event as "triggering the libs." They claimed that liberals see white supremacy in benign symbols, and OK was just OK, even though they themselves claimed it stood for white people.[7] Shortly thereafter, the Anti-Defamation League and the Southern Poverty Law Center declared the gesture a symbol of hate.[8] Both organizations went to great lengths to explain that it was contextual and not every instance of the OK gesture symbolized allegiance with white supremacy. This visibility helped increase its use among real white supremacists, further establishing its connection to hate.

---

[5]Neiwert; "Okay Hand Gesture"; Staff, "What the 'OK' Hand Signal Means for the Militia Movement."

[6]4Chan is a social media site where users can anonymously post anything. Users do not have to make an account to post, and posts are temporary, so there is zero accountability for anything said or done.

[7]Neiwert, "Is That an OK Sign?"

[8]Staff, "What the 'OK' Hand Signal Means for the Militia Movement"; "Okay Hand Gesture."

However, the OK hand shape isn't doomed: it can also be overwhelmingly positive, representing teaching in Buddhist contexts, and love in Ancient Greece (because the fingers kiss). It can also represent enlightenment, or perfection. Obviously, these meanings are much older and more globally familiar than OK as a symbol of hate or degradation.

But as with most words, most of the functions of the gesture are neither positive nor negative and only works to do what gestures normally do: facilitate communication. For example, in Japan, money can be socially awkward to discuss (especially in the case of a bribe or other illicit financial transaction), so the gesture helps fill in the gaps, indicating that money will be exchanged.[9] Between divers, communication is difficult but essential, so the OK gesture has been codified as both a question and response: "Are you OK?", "Yes, I'm OK, are you OK?" (the thumb up was already taken to signal going up).

But, just like the word, the OK gesture is understood in context. Even in cultures that have pre-existing connotations for the OK hand shape, the American OK is widely recognized. For example, in the south of France, it typically refers to zero while in the north, the more common interpretation is OK. But in both regions, context is crucial and the American reading can be just as easily evoked as the French one. But even

---

[9]Müller, "Ring-Gestures across Cultures and Times."

in an American context, it can communicate OK, and it can also represent a small or precise amount of something.

So where did the OK hand gesture come from, and how did such a young word earn itself a gesture? There are actually a few creation myths for this hand shape. The first—which a lot of people just assume—is that it derives from the American Sign Language manual alphabet for /o/ and /k/. Since /k/ in ASL is made with the index finger raised, middle finger half raised, and other fingers tucked, this is just incorrect.

The next theory is that it was used at the Democratic O.K. Clubs in the early 1840s. However, there is no evidence that the hand shape was in active use there or that it had any political connection (before it was co-opted by white supremacists around 2015). Most likely this hypothesis results from confusion between the origin of the word OK and the origin of the hand shape.[10]

Finally, there is the precision origin. This is the most plausible, and states that OK derives from the hand gesture for precision. The argument is that in almost every culture, when talking about precision, people use a ring gesture, as if they are holding something very small between their index finger and thumb. As the thinking goes, in the United States, the other fingers were held relatively straight and apart and— over time—this hand shape was amplified into a deliberate symbol for perfection or all correct.[11]

---

[10]Wagner and Armstrong. *The field guide to gestures.*
[11]Morris, *Peoplewatching.*

However, because gestures are not as well documented as text, it is difficult to pinpoint exactly when the OK hand gesture started meaning OK. The best explanation is that in the United States, the gesture evolved from the precision hand shape sometime after OK was lexicalized, placing it early twentieth century. It may have been slightly earlier, possibly getting its start with the railroads as there may have been need for gestural communication and OK was wildly popular among railroad engineers. Regardless, by the mid-twentieth century, the OK gesture was widely understood both in and out of the United States.

Telecommunications and globalization helped make the gesture mean OK in a shockingly short period of time. Every invention, connection, and twist of fate that spread OK as a word spread OK as a hand gesture. Every force that positioned the United States as a cultural influencer brought American language—and gesture—with it.

But the OK hand gesture is not the only gesture or icon making its way around the world. In the years since the gesture was codified, a whole new way of communicating was invented: emojis. Emojis were invented by two Japanese telephone companies: J-Phone in 1997 and again by DoCoMo in 1999.[12] The DoCoMo ones are the precursor to

---

[12]DoCoMo is a Japanese company, but the name stands for "Do communications over the mobile-network," an English phrase made Japanese through creative abbreviation.

the modern emoji set. The goal of DoCoMo was to convey information, and the earliest emojis reflect that goal: there were clouds and sunshine, but faces and the OK gestures were missing.

Today, it is the international Unicode consortium who determines which emojis will be made available. The consortium was established in 1991 to standardize the way emojis are encoded, and every year, they vote on new emoji proposals. In 2010, the Unicode consortium released a major overhaul of emoji in an effort to provide compatibility for the way emoji were being rendered worldwide. The OK hand gesture appeared in that 2010 update and has been relatively unchanged ever since.

With the formalization into an emoji, the OK hand gesture has become even more widespread, existing beyond in speaking, writing, and gesture into emoji. Some say that emoji is becoming a universal language, but the question remains: Whose language, and whose standard is universal?

11 O.K. OK, OK, LOL . . . (CONCLUSION)

When I was writing this book, I told people that I was writing a book about the word, OK, and—without fail—every single person replied with "OK . . ." in tones that expressed various levels of curiosity, incredulity, and enthusiasm. Every. Single. Person. Young, old, monolingual, bilingual, urban, rural, across the education spectrum, it didn't matter—everyone started their next sentence with OK.

That level of linguistic homogeneity is shocking. When we take into consideration the linguistic diversity of this group, it is utterly mind boggling. There are, of course, other appropriate responses to my statement: "Hmmm," "Cool," "Oh, really?" But no one used them. This brings us to the last lesson that OK holds, one about how we all start using the same words, and a process called linguistic convergence.

People who spend a lot of time together start to sound like each other. We might meet a new friend who says like a lot, and before we know it, we're saying like, too. Or we might start dating someone who describes everything as funky and suddenly we describe those great shoes as funky, too. We experience this when we make new friends, start new romantic relationships, even when we start new jobs. But it isn't limited to verbal speech; this happens just as much in conversational writing (like text messaging or chat). For example, we might start a new job where people write "lol" in their messages and just a couple weeks later, lol starts creeping into ours, too. The interesting bit is that it's not just limited to that person. Eventually, those new words or expressions make their way into our vocabulary and we're lol'ing people we never lol'd before. This behavior—where one person shifts their language to match another's—is linguistic convergence.

Linguistic convergence is the unsung hero of language change. It happens slowly, person-to-person and is the gentle spreading of a word through a society that helps us understand each other. But it's a slow process: convergence happens during interaction and requires actively engaging with others and trading language. It's the natural flow of language and stands in stark contrast to forces like virality.

Virality happens like a spark: suddenly large numbers of people have focused their attention on something, but then it fades away. Videos, memes, and other media go viral easily in a digitally connected word, and words do, too. For example, there's "botax," a 2009 candidate for the American Dialect Society's word of the year, that means a tax levied on cosmetic procedures. Or a candidate from 2018: "orbiting," which means ending communication with someone while still monitoring them on social media.[1] Just like OK, they were creative adaptations to describe something culturally relevant for the time. Unlike OK, they never became part of the English vocabulary.

We can find reasons for this: maybe it's because OK is more universally applicable or maybe it's easier to understand, but those reasons are just speculations. In the end, no one knows why OK caught on and orbiting didn't. What we do know is that OK spread because people used it. That is what linguistic convergence is all about: people using language. It's the gentle changes to how we communicate that is in the hands of everyone who participates; it's the force at the center of all language change.

The great moments of creativity, brilliant political slogans, and world-changing inventions are easy to identify and stand out as turning points. But the incredible thing about language is not those bright moments of change—it's that language is created during every single human interaction. OK is no exception. The technologies that shaped it only provided the platform. In the end, it was always people who made the language.

OK teaches us a lesson about the alliance between our humanity and technology. OK was invented during a stroke of creativity and playfulness, some of the best human characteristics. But it's existence is completely dependent

---

[1] American Dialect Society, Word of the Year

on writing, publishing, and market forces, each a powerful technology. OK spread because technology spread, but stayed alive because humans have an innate desire to communicate. Language in a literate society is both biological and technological, and OK symbolizes that dichotomy, born of technology, and spread by biology (and vice versa).

True to form, that's not the only dichotomy OK embodies. It describes both good and bad, offers both approval and hesitation, changes a topic and keeps it going, can be written formally and creatively, and fills almost any kind of purpose when needed. With just two letters, OK contains multitudes.

BIBLIOGRAPHY

Alcott, Louisa May. *Little Women*. New York: Signet Classic, 2004.

American Dialect Society, "Word of the Year." January 4, 2019. https://www.americandialect.org/woty.

Aston, Nigel. "The Newspaper Press in the French Revolution." *The Historical Journal* 33, no. 4 (December 1, 1990): 1003.

Baron, Naomi. "Instant Messaging and the Future of Language." *Communications of the ACM*, July 2005.

Beauchamp, Christopher. "Who Invented the Telephone? Lawyers, Patents, and the Judgments of History." *Technology and Culture* 51, no. 4 (2010): 854–78.

Brown, Travis. *Historical First Patents: The First United States Patent for Many Everyday Things*. Metuchen, N.J.: Scarecrow Press, 1994.

Bush, Randy. "FidoNet: Technology, Use, Tools, and History." FidoNet, 1992. http://www.fidonet.org/inet92_Randy_Bush.txt.

Cassidy, Frederic G. "OK. Is It African?" *American Speech* 56, no. 4 (1981): 269–73. https://doi.org/10.2307/455123.

"Chronicling America Temporal Coverage (Entire Collection) - *Chronicling America: Historic American Newspapers*." Accessed March 19, 2020. https://public.tableau.com/profile/chronicling .america#!/vizhome/ChroniclingAmericaTemporalCoverageE ntireCollection/TemporalCoverage.

Cohen, Ronald D. "The School upon a Hill: Education and Society in Colonial New England." *History: Reviews of New Books*

3, no. 4 (February 1, 1975): 92–92. https://doi.org/10.1080/03612759.1975.9946800.

Control, Connecticut Board of Finance and. *The Budget Report of the State Board of Finance and Control to the General Assembly, Session of [1929-] 1937*. The State., 1901.

Crystal, David. "English Worldwide." In *A History of the English Language*, edited by David Denison and Richard Hogg, 420–39. Cambridge: Cambridge University Press, 2006. https://doi.org/10.1017/CBO9780511791154.010.

Crystal, David. "The History of English." *Voices by the BBC,* Nov. 2004. https://www.bbc.co.uk/voices/yourvoice/feature2_2.shtml.

Dalby, David. "O.K., A.O.K. and O KE." *New York Times*, January 8, 1971, sec. Archives. https://www.nytimes.com/1971/01/08/archives/ok-aok-and-o-ke-the-remarkable-career-of-an-americanism-that-began.html.

Edel, L. "MO_ICONS_PLEASE." *FidoNet* (blog), May 8, 1989. http://www.textfiles.com/fidonet-on-the-internet/878889/fido0619.txt.

Evans, M. D. R., Jonathan Kelley, and Joanna Sikora. "Scholarly Culture and Academic Performance in 42 Nations." *Social Forces* 92, no. 4 (June 1, 2014): 1573–1605. https://doi.org/10.1093/sf/sou030.

Feather, John. *A History of British Publishing*. Taylor & Francis, 2006.

Fischer, Claude S. *America Calling: A Social History of the Telephone to 1940*. University of California Press, 1994.

Freehling, William. "William Harrison: Campaigns and Elections | Miller Center," October 4, 2016. https://millercenter.org/president/harrison/campaigns-and-elections.

Garson, Robert, and Charles W. Kegley. "The Rise and Rise of American Exceptionalism." Edited by Sanford J. et al. *Review of International Studies* 16, no. 2 (1990): 173–79.

Gonçalves, Bruno, Lucía Loureiro-Porto, José J. Ramasco, and David Sánchez. "Mapping the Americanization of English in Space and Time." *PLOS ONE* 13, no. 5 (May 25, 2018): e0197741. https://doi.org/10.1371/journal.pone.0197741.

Gross, Robert A., and Matt Cohen. "Building a National Literature." In *A Companion to the History of the Book*, 499–514. John Wiley & Sons, Ltd, 2019. https://doi.org/10.1002/9781119018193.ch33.

Grubb, F. W. "Growth of Literacy in Colonial America: Longitudinal Patterns, Economic Models, and the Direction of Future Research." *Social Science History* 14, no. 4 (1990): 451–82. https://doi.org/10.2307/1171328.

Hammond, C.A. "The Railroad Telephone." In Monthly Bulletin: *(English Edition)*. P. Weissenbruch, 1902.

Harper, Lawrence A. "Mercantilism and the American Revolution." *The Canadian Historical Review* 23, no. 1 (1942): 1–15.

Hatewatch Staff. "What the "OK" Hand Signal Means for the Militia Movement." *Hatewatch, Southern Poverty Law Center*, June 12, 2017. https://www.splcenter.org/hatewatch/2017/06/12/what-ok-hand-signal-means-militia-movement.

Health, Indiana State Board of. *Annual Report of the State Board of Health of Indiana*. State Board of Health, 1909.

Jurafsky, Daniel. "Universal Tendencies in the Semantics of the Diminutive." *Language* 72, no. 3 (1996): 533–78. https://doi.org/10.2307/416278.

King, Andrew. ""Literature of the Kitchen": Cheap Serial Fiction of the 1840s and 1850s." In *A Companion to Sensation Fiction*, 38–53. John Wiley & Sons, Ltd, 2011. https://doi.org/10.1002/9781444342239.ch3.

Kinstler, Linda. "Finding Lena, the Patron Saint of JPEGs." *Wired*, (January 13, 2019). https://www.wired.com/story/finding-lena-the-patron-saint-of-jpegs/

Labov, Teresa. "Social and Language Boundaries among Adolescents." *American Speech* 67, no. 4 (1992): 339–66. https://doi.org/10.2307/455845.

Leiner, Barry M., Vinton G. Cerf, David D. Clark, Robert E. Kahn, Leonard Kleinrock, Daniel C. Lynch, Jon Postel, Larry G. Roberts, and Stephen Wolff. "A Brief History of the Internet." *ACM SIGCOMM Computer Communication Review* 39, no. 5 (October 7, 2009): 22–31. https://doi.org/10.1145/1629607.1629613.

Mahajan, Sanjoy. "Were Colonial Americans More Literate than Americans Today?" *Freakonomics* (blog), September 1, 2011. https://freakonomics.com/2011/09/01/were-colonial-americans-more-literate-than-americans-today/.

Marvin, Carolyn. *When Old Technologies Were New: Thinking About Electric Communication in the Late Nineteenth Century*. Oxford University Press, 1990.

McGregor, Jena, William C. Symonds, and Dean Foust. "How Failure Breeds Success." *Business Week* 10 (2006).

McSweeney, Michelle. "Bilingual Youth Texts Corpus," 2016. www.byts.commons.gc.cuny.edu.

McSweeney, Michelle. *The Pragmatics of Text Messaging: Making Meaning in Messages*. 1 edition. New York: Routledge, 2018.

Mencken, H. L. *American Language*. Knopf Doubleday Publishing Group, 1936.

Mencken, H. L. *The American Language Supplement 1*. Knopf Doubleday Publishing Group, 1945.

Merchant, Guy. "Teenagers in Cyberspace: An Investigation of Language Use and Language Change in Internet Chatrooms." *Journal of Research in Reading* 24, no. 3 (2001): 293–306.

Metcalf, Allan. *OK: The Improbable Story of America's Greatest Word*. Oxford, New York: Oxford University Press, 2010.

Moffett, Samuel Erasmus. *The Americanization of Canada*. Columbia University, 1907.

Morris, Desmond. *Peoplewatching: The Desmond Morris Guide to Body Language.* Random House, 2012.

Murphey. 1838. *Murphey's Weather Almanac, for the Year 1839.* Fifth Edition. G. Gilbert.

Müller, Cornelia. "Ring-Gestures across Cultures and Times: Dimensions of Variation." Berlin, München, Boston: DE GRUYTER, 2014. https://doi.org/10.1515/9783110302028.1511.

Nerone, John C. "The Mythology of the Penny Press." *Critical Studies in Mass Communication* 4, no. 4 (December 1, 1987): 376–404. https://doi.org/10.1080/15295038709360146.

New York and Erie Railroad Company. Annual Report, 1856.

Anti-Defamation League. "Okay Hand Gesture." Accessed March 29, 2021. https://www.adl.org/education/references/hate-symbols/okay-hand-gesture.

Paolillo, John C. ""Conversational" Codeswitching on Usenet and Internet Relay Chat." *Language@Internet* 8, no. 3 (December 24, 2011). http://www.languageatinternet.org/articles/2011/3214.

Pearson's Magazine. C. Arthur Pearson Limited, 1896.

Pennycook, Alastair. *English and the Discourses of Colonialism.* Psychology Press, 1998.

Puttnam, David. *Movies and Money.* Knopf Doubleday Publishing Group, 2011.

Read, Allen Walker. "Could Andrew Jackson Spell?" *American Speech* 38, no. 3 (1963): 188–95. https://doi.org/10.2307/454098.

Read, Allen Walker. "The First Stage in the History of "O. K."" *American Speech* 38, no. 1 (1963): 5–27. https://doi.org/10.2307/453580.

Read, Allen Walker. "The Folklore of "O. K."" *American Speech* 39, no. 1 (1964): 5–25. https://doi.org/10.2307/453922.

Read, Allen Walker. "The Second Stage in the History of "O. K."" *American Speech* 38, no. 2 (May 1963): 21.

Reisen, Harriet. *Louisa May Alcott: The Woman Behind Little Women*. Henry Holt and Company, 2009.

Saunders, E. Dale. "Symbolic Gestures in Buddhism." *Artibus Asiae* 21, no. 1 (1958): 47–63.

Schivelbusch, Wolfgang. *The Railway Journey: The Industrialization of Time and Space in the Nineteenth Century*. Univ of California Press, 1986. https://books.google.com/books?hl=en&lr= &id=YzuJAwAAQBAJ&oi=fnd&pg=PP1&dq=schivelbusch +railway+journey&ots=vvftJLfQsI&sig=t_vpoKIAgs73adsBT _Fvtpy5nSg.

Stamp, Robert M. "Educational Thought and Educational Practice during the Years of the French Revolution." *History of Education Quarterly* 6, no. 3 (1966): 35–49. https://doi.org/10 .2307/367620.

Wagnleitner, Reinhold. *Coca-Colonization and the Cold War: The Cultural Mission of the United States in Austria After the Second World War*. Univ of North Carolina Press, 2000.

Walden's Stationer and Printer, 1907.

INDEX

OBJECT LESSONS

Cross them all off your list.

exit
LAURA WADDELL

9781501358159

gin
SHONNA MILLIKEN HUMPHREY

9781501353277

snake
ERICA WRIGHT

9781501348716

bulletproof vest
KENNETH R. ROSEN

9781501353024

coffee
DINAH LENNEY

9781501344350

environment
ROLF HALDEN

9781501361906

"Perfect for slipping in a pocket and pulling out when life is on hold."

– Toronto Star

9781501353352

9781501348815

9781501348518

9781501348631

9781501325991

9781501307409